Earth and Space
Nick England and Rosalind Jones

CONTENTS

Earth and Atmosphere
1. Weather and Atmosphere 2
2. The Water Cycle 4
3. Prevailing Winds 6
4. Highs and Lows 8
5. Weathering, Erosion and Transport 12
6. The Rock Cycle 14
7. The Structure of the Earth 16
8. Plate Tectonics 20
9. Evidence for Plate Tectonics 23

Earth and Space
10. The Solar System 26
11. The Four Seasons 28
12. Beyond the Solar System 30
13. Moving Planets 32
14. Gravitation 34
15. Making a Star 36
16. The Hertzsprung-Russell Diagram 38
17. The Planets 40
18. Sun, Stand Still! 43
19. Origins 46

Things To Do 48
Activities 54
Index 64

1 WEATHER AND ATMOSPHERE

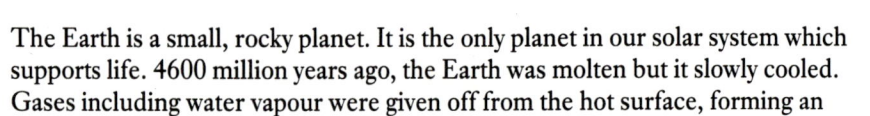

The Earth is a small, rocky planet. It is the only planet in our solar system which supports life. 4600 million years ago, the Earth was molten but it slowly cooled. Gases including water vapour were given off from the hot surface, forming an atmosphere. Eventually, the Earth cooled enough for water to collect on its surface.

Weather and climate

We all take an interest in the weather, particularly in the UK where the weather sometimes changes from one hour to the next. **Weather** is the state of the atmosphere at any one time or place. It includes the temperature, rainfall, windspeed and wind direction. **Climate**, on the other hand, is the average of these weather records over a long period of time.

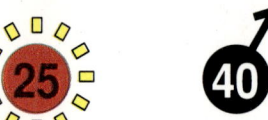
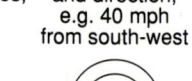

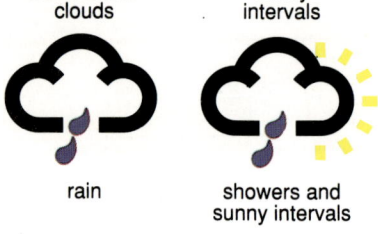

Figure 1
TV weather symbols

The weather affects our daily lives. Many people try to watch the weather report on television every day. This is Ian McCaskill from the Meteorological Office giving a weather report. He is using standard symbols to explain the weather

Information about the weather is collected from weather stations on land and sea, from weather balloons and from satellites which view the Earth from space. They provide the vital basis for weather forecasts. There are various ways to describe the weather. The symbols used on television weather maps are shown in Figure 1. You can see some of these in the photograph too.

EARTH AND SPACE

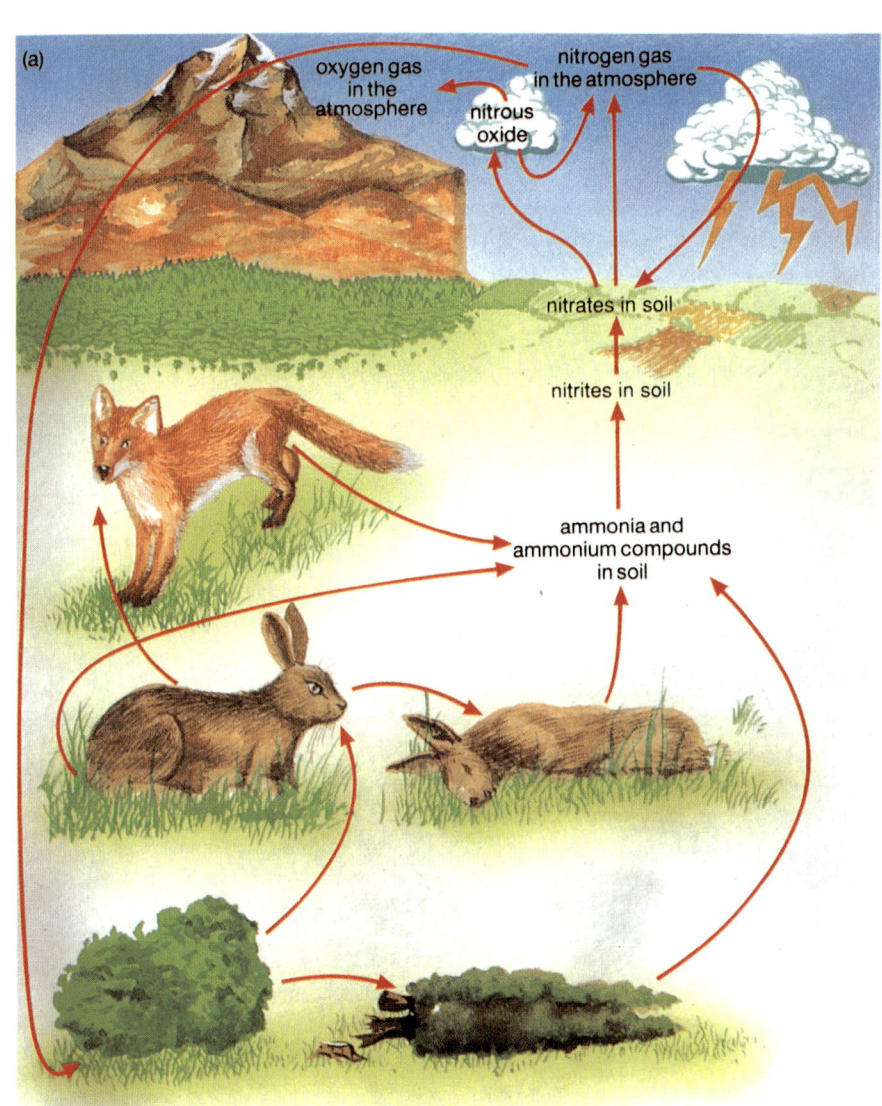

Figure 2
Gaseous cycles in the atmosphere
(a) Circulation of nitrogen and ammonia
(b) Circulation of carbon and methane

The evolution of our atmosphere

4600 million years ago, the Earth was still forming. At first, the atmosphere was rich in hydrogen and helium. As the molten, volcanically active surface cooled, other gases were added. These included methane, carbon dioxide and water vapour. When simple, green plants appeared 3500 million years ago, oxygen was formed from carbon dioxide by photosynthesis. Gradually complex plants evolved, adding more oxygen to the atmosphere. In time, animals evolved and used the oxygen for respiration. This helped to maintain a balance between the production and use of both oxygen and carbon dioxide. The composition of the atmosphere has remained more or less in balance for the last 500 million years.

Today, our industries are altering this delicate balance. Burning fossil fuels in excess of the quantity plants can cope with is removing oxygen and adding more carbon dioxide to the atmosphere. The clearing of forests has also resulted in a decrease in oxygen production by photosynthesis. Figure 2 shows how air is renewed by living creatures. Nitrogen, oxygen and carbon dioxide are used and restored to the soil and atmosphere in their cycles.

QUESTIONS

1 What measurements are always taken at a weather station?

2 (a) Using the weather symbols in Figure 1, record your own observations of the weather for today. Write a paragraph to record these same conditions in the kind of language used in weather forecasts.

(b) Use the television symbols to plot your own weather map for the British Isles for a cold, windy winter day.

2 THE WATER CYCLE

The Water Cycle

The never-ending circulation of the Earth's water supply is called the water cycle, or **Hydrological Cycle**. The watery layer of ocean, lakes and rivers which covers most of the Earth's surface, called the **hydrosphere**, was originally formed thousands of millions of years ago, as the Earth cooled. Water was gradually released from the solidifying crust as vapour, which rose into the atmosphere, cooled and condensed, and fell back to the Earth's surface as rain. Eventually this rain water formed the Earth's oceans which today cover 60% of our planet.

Oceans hold by far the most water on the planet, and are the beginning and end of the water cycle. The atmosphere and the land hold water in the intermediate stages of this huge system, which is powered by heat energy from the Sun. The atmosphere forms the link in the cycle between the oceans (which contain 97% of the Earth's water), and the continents (which contain almost 3%). A diagram of the water cycle is shown in Figure 1, which shows how the whole thing works.

Water evaporates from oceans and the land when energy from the Sun heats the surface. The vapour rises into the atmosphere, where it forms tiny droplets which are transported as moist air by the wind. As more droplets collect, and join up to form larger droplets, clouds eventually form. If the clouds move over the sea from the land, or rise up over a mountain, the drop in temperature causes the droplets to condense into larger drops. Because the drops are too heavy to stay in the atmosphere, they fall as rain, hail, sleet or snow. Most of this **precipitation** falls back into the oceans, and will begin the cycle again. A smaller amount falls on the continents, from where it gradually makes its way back to the oceans. Some precipitation which falls onto land sinks, or **infiltrates** into the soil, while some becomes **run-off**, which flows over the surface, joins the **drainage system** of streams and rivers and flows back to the ocean. Water which infiltrates into soil, and then into rock, becomes **groundwater**, which eventually joins streams and becomes part of run-off. Some groundwater flows directly into the sea.

Figure 1
The water cycle

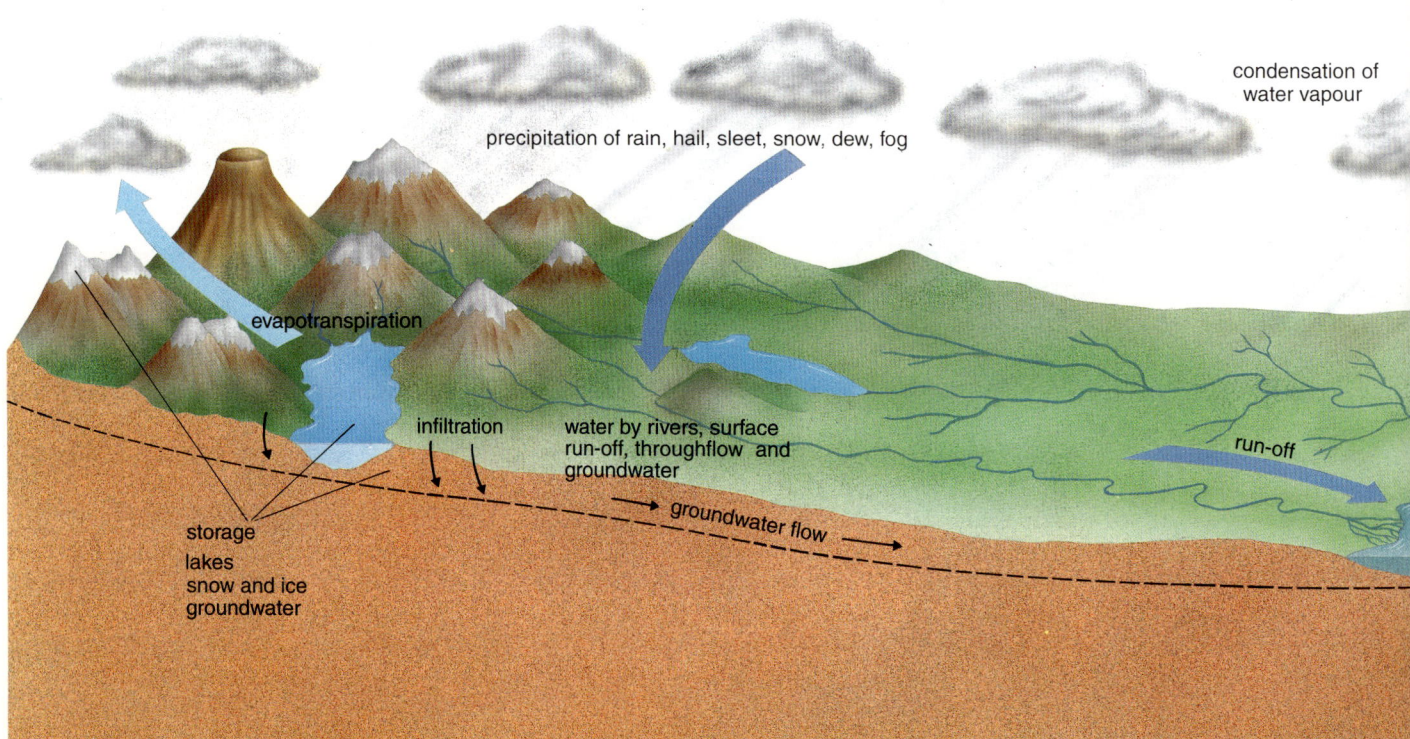

Snow or hail may stay frozen in cold continental areas. A great deal of fresh water is stored in snow fields and glaciers, though some is released as meltwater or vapour when temperatures get high enough. A lot of water which infiltrates or runs off the surface of the land is evaporated back to the atmosphere before it reaches the ocean, while some is taken up by plants and is lost during transpiration. When water goes back into the atmosphere by evaporation and transpiration we call this **evapotranspiration**.

Oceans lose more water by evaporation into the atmosphere than they receive from precipitation. Continents receive more precipitation from the atmosphere than they lose by evaporation. It is the flow of run-off water and groundwater that balance the cycle, as shown in Figure 1.

Mist, fog, dew and frost

During the day, surface water evaporates from oceans, rivers and even puddles into the atmosphere. The water absorbs heat from the atmosphere as it evaporates, which results in a general cooling of the air. If the air temperature falls a little further, tiny droplets of water condense again, and a mist forms in the atmosphere. If the air temperature drops even further, more water droplets condense, the mist gets thicker and we call this fog. If the temperature of the ground falls at the same time, then water condenses at ground level as dew. As the vapour condenses, heat energy is released which warms the atmosphere.

Frost forms when the temperature of the ground and the atmosphere falls below 0°C. Particularly on starry nights with no cloud to prevent heat loss by radiation, the air quickly falls below 0°C and moisture forms needle-shaped ice crystals.

Water molecules turn to ice crystals if the temperature drops below freezing. The frost in this photo is an example. Water may become trapped in cracks in solid material such as rocks or building stone. If this water freezes, its expansion can cause breakages in the rock or stone

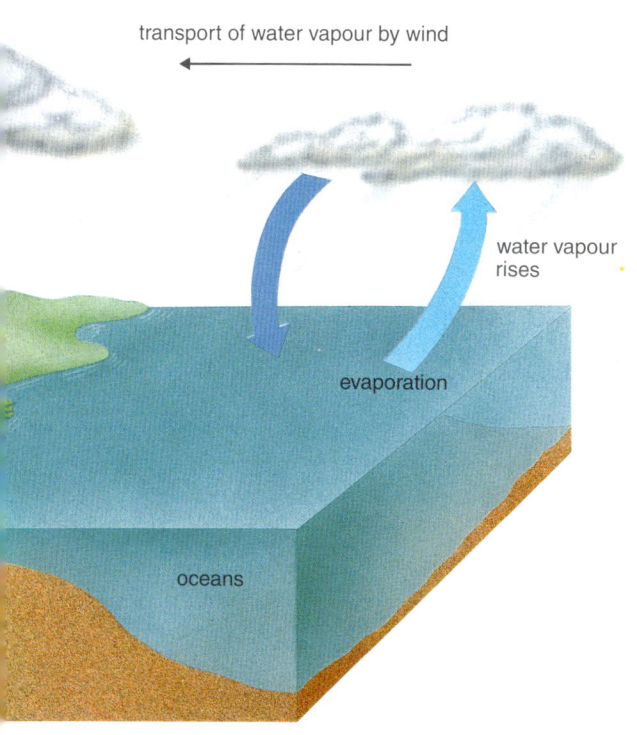

QUESTIONS

1 Explain carefully the difference between water droplets and water vapour.
2 Describe and explain the conditions that are necessary for the formation of fog.
3 The highest rainfall in England is in Seathwaite, which lies about five kilometres east of the Scafell range of mountains; explain this.
4 Why is the annual average rainfall greater near the equator than it is in Britain?

3 PREVAILING WINDS

The Sun is the Earth's source of energy. As well as supporting life, solar energy controls our planet's climate and weather. As the Earth remains at a fairly steady temperature, there must be a balance between incoming energy (**solar radiation**) and outgoing heat loss (**terrestrial radiation**). 45% of the solar radiation reaches the Earth's surface. 55% of the energy is absorbed and re-emitted by the atmosphere.

The surface of the Earth is not warmed evenly; the equator receives far more radiation than the poles. However the equator only radiates a little more into space than the poles, because the temperature of space is close to absolute zero (Figure 1). This imbalance would cause the equator to become unbearably hot, if it were not for the fact that energy is carried away by convection currents. Most of the energy is carried by airstreams, though ocean currents (such as the Gulf Stream) also contribute to the transfer of energy towards the poles.

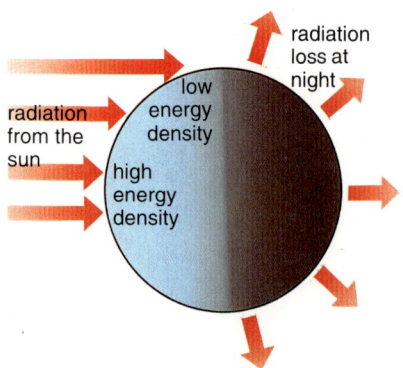

Figure 1
Heat budget for the Earth: an imbalance in radiation density creates a hot equator and cold poles

Global airstreams

The airstreams, or global winds, are convection currents on a very large scale. Warm, less dense air rises, and cold, denser air flows in to replace it. Powered by the Sun airstreams circulate constantly between the hot tropics and the freezing poles. Figure 2 shows how air might circulate on a slowly rotating Earth, but the Earth's rotation produces two major effects: first the air flow is broken up into three **cells**, and secondly the airstreams are deflected away from a northwards or southwards flow.

Figure 3 shows the global airstreams over one quarter of the globe. Hot air rising from the equator creates the **doldrums**, an area of low pressure and light, variable winds. As the air rises it cools and spreads outwards, then becomes denser and sinks. Belts of high pressure and relative calm, which we call **horse latitudes**, result from this movement of air. The dense, high pressure air at the horse latitudes flows back towards the equator. This circular flow of a large mass of air is known as a cell. Some air from the tropical cells flows towards the temperate latitudes, creating **mid latitude cells**, which end where **polar cells** of very cold air flow away from the poles, displacing the warm air. The cold polar air warms up in the temperate latitudes, rises and flows back to the poles where it cools and sinks again. Wind blows from regions of high pressure to regions of low pressure; for example, winds tend to blow from the high pressure areas in the horse latitudes to the lower pressure areas in the temperate latitudes.

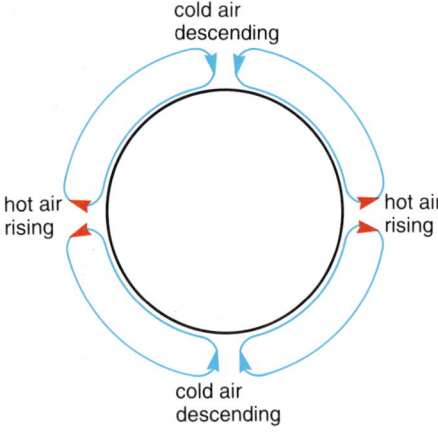

Figure 2
If the Earth rotated very slowly, heat would be carried away from the equator by simple convection currents such as those shown here

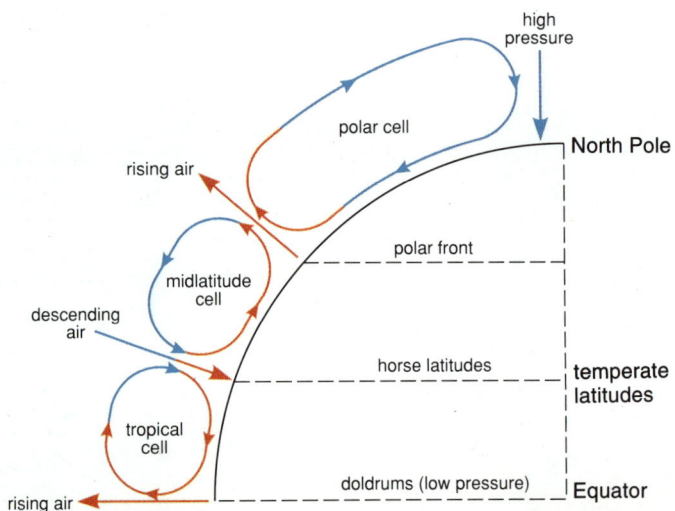

Figure 3

Coriolis effect

The Earth rotates as a solid body. This means that the equator is moving faster than the surface of the Earth at higher latitudes. As a result of this airstreams are deflected east or west as they move over the Earth's surface, this is called the **Coriolis effect**. Hot air which rises from the equator has an eastwards velocity of about 1700 km/h, but air at a latitude of 30°N only has an eastwards velocity of about 1500 km/h.

Therefore the hot air overtakes the air at higher latitudes and is deflected eastwards. On the other hand, cold air travelling southwards is deflected towards the west, since it is travelling more slowly than the more southerly air. The winds in the northern tropical cell travel towards the south west. Winds are named after the direction from which they blow, so these are the north-east trade winds. In the horse latitudes, cold air travelling northwards is deflected towards the east to produce the prevailing south westerlies.

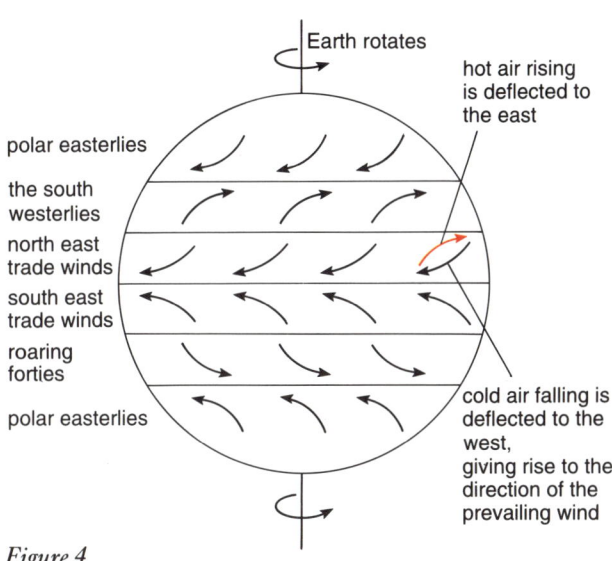

Figure 4
The Earth's prevailing winds

Jupiter

QUESTIONS

1 The Moon's surface reaches a temperature of 150°C, when sunlight falls on it, yet during the lunar night the Moon's surface temperature drops to −150°C. The Moon and Earth are the same distance away from the Sun, but the hottest and coldest recorded temperatures on Earth are 50°C and −90°C. Account for the differences between the lunar and terrestrial temperatures.

2 (a) Explain how convective cells arise on the Earth.
(b) Why is there more than one convective cell in each hemisphere?

3 In the northern hemisphere the trade winds blow from the north east, but in the southern hemisphere they blow from the south east. Explain why.

4 Look at the photograph of Jupiter. The dark bands are called belts; these are regions of gas low down in the atmosphere. The lighter bands are called zones; these are higher in the atmosphere than the belts and are colder. Jupiter has a diameter 11 times that of the Earth, and it completes one revolution on its axis in 10 hours.

(a) Explain how these belts and bands might be formed.
(b) Why do you think that there are more belts on Jupiter than there are convective cells on the Earth?
(c) Atmospheric features near the equator of Jupiter have been observed moving at several hundreds of kilometres per hour. Account for these very large Jovian wind speeds.
(d) Such large wind speeds give rise to turbulence. What features in Jupiter's atmosphere could be due to turbulence?

4 HIGHS AND LOWS

Air masses affecting the British Isles

Weather around the world is controlled by a number of air masses, which originate from source regions. Such regions are found in areas dominated by large semi-permanent high pressure systems. These are often associated with the interiors of large land masses, for example: northern Canada, Siberia and the Arctic Basin in winter. In summer, desert areas such as the Sahara, central Asia and central America, produce large masses of warm, dry air.

Figure 1 shows the routes followed by the five main air masses which affect the British Isles. We live on the eastern edge of the Atlantic Ocean, in a region where prevailing westerly winds have collected moisture during their long passage over the sea. Our weather is dominated by two maritime air masses, polar and tropical.

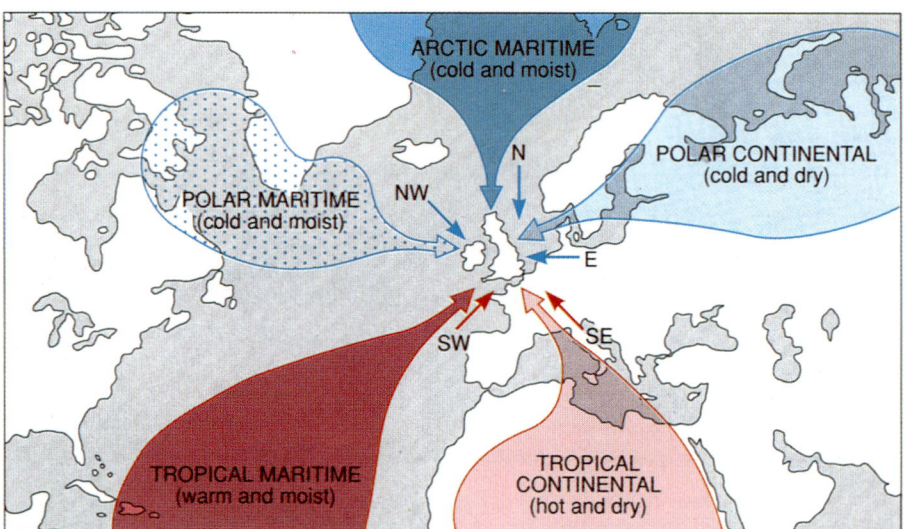

Figure 1
The air masses that affect the British Isles

- Polar maritime air has its source in the North Atlantic Ocean south of Greenland. This air mass occupies Britain for nearly half the year in all seasons. This air brings with it cool and very moist air, which is associated with short-lived but heavy showers.
- Tropical maritime air, coming from the high pressure system near the Azores, controls our weather for about 15% of the year in all seasons. When the air leaves its source region it is warm and moist, and the skies are clear. Often the air mass can bring the same pleasant weather with it to the British Isles, but sometimes the air is cooled in its passage northwards and heavy thunderstorms can be the result in the summer.
- Polar continental air is less common over the British Isles, only affecting us as a rule during the winter months. Cold, dry air originates over Siberia and it brings with it clear skies, which allow a lot of heat to be radiated away into space overnight. This weather is typified by bitter cold and severe frosts.
- Arctic air is rare over Britain. It starts as Arctic continental air but after its long journey south it picks up some moisture, although cold air cannot hold as much water vapour as warmer air. These air streams can bring heavy snow showers in the north and on high ground.
- Tropical continental air is also rare; this reaches us from North Africa. These air masses are very stable and can lead to long heat waves, such as the summer we experienced in 1976.

Anticyclones

In the mid-latitudes where we live there are two types of **anticyclone** or high pressure system. One type is an extension of the polar continental or tropical continental high pressure cells. The second type is interspersed with low pressure systems moving in with maritime air masses. Atmospheric pressure increases towards the centre of an anticyclone. This causes the air to fall outwards in a descending spiral, rather like water going down the bath plug. As the air falls it warms up, which suppresses the formation of clouds. Therefore high pressure systems bring with them clear skies. The pressure gradient in the air is small, so the isobars are widely spaced and the winds are light; they blow in a clockwise direction around the centre of the system, in the northern hemisphere. You can see these features in the weather map shown in Figure 2.

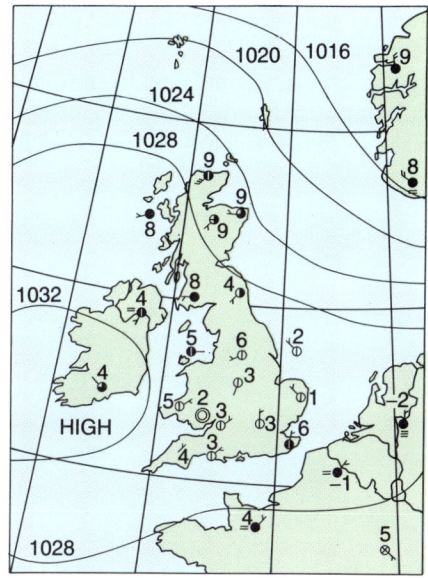

Figure 2
High pressure region over Britain. This anticyclone has pushed northwards from north Africa, bringing with it clear skies and hot, calm weather. The pressure on our weather maps is measured in millibars: 1 millibar = 100 Nm^{-2}

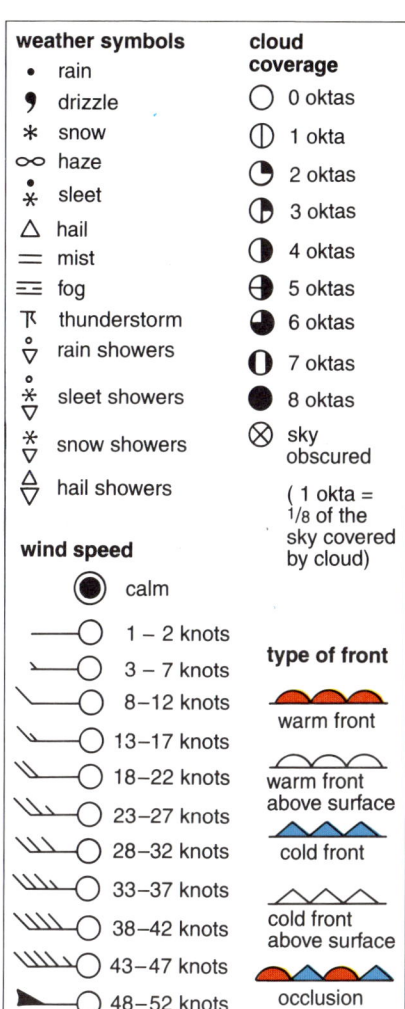

Figure 3
'Synoptic symbols' used for Met Office weather maps. Why do you think TV weather maps used different symbols?

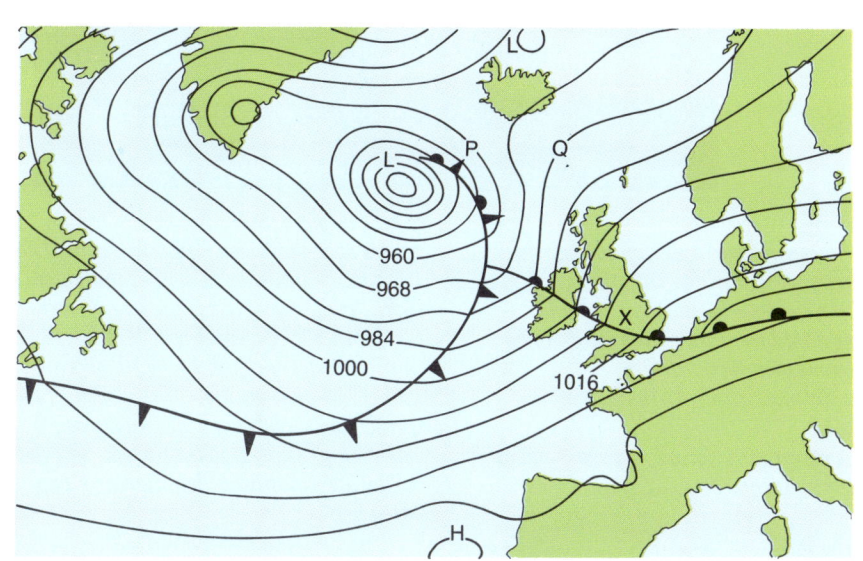

Figure 4
A frontal system moves over Britain

HIGHS AND LOWS

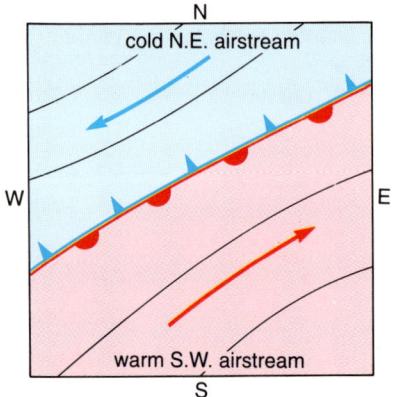

(a)

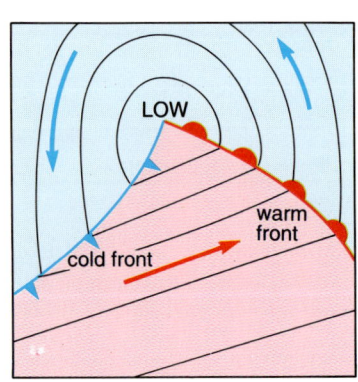

(b)

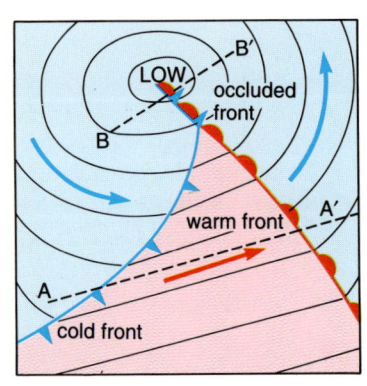

(c)

(d)

Depressions

In Britain we are all familiar with a **depression**, **cyclone** or low pressure system; usually these have frontal systems associated with them. The series of diagrams in Figure 3 shows how such a system arises.

- In diagram (a) a warm south westerly air stream meets a cold polar air mass travelling from the north east.
- In diagram (b) the warm air has begun to bulge northwards into the colder air. Distinct warm and cold fronts have now been formed, which begin to rotate around a centre of low pressure.
- By diagram (c) a deep central depression has been formed; low pressure air spirals upwards cooling as it rises. Cloud formation occurs as rising water vapour in the atmosphere cools and condenses. Heavy rain is associated with frontal systems. There is a strong pressure gradient and strong winds circulate in an anticlockwise direction (in the northern hemisphere) around the centre of the depression. The system moves westwards towards the British Isles.
- In diagram (d) of the sequence the warm air has been squeezed upwards to leave an **occluded front**. It is quite hard to visualise the nature of frontal systems using just views from above. Figure 6 shows two cross-sections through fronts in Figure 5(d).

Figure 5
(a) Polar continental and tropical maritime air masses meet over the Atlantic Ocean
(b) The air masses begin to curl around, forming a cold front travelling south and a warm front moving north
(c) The air masses spiral around a central depression
(d) The warm air is forced upwards, and an occluded front is formed

A false colour satellite image of a frontal system over the North Atlantic Ocean. The UK and France may be seen at the bottom right. At the top centre is the ice cap over Greenland. The frontal system is the swirling mass of clouds to the left of centre, with a low pressure area at the centre of the spiral. Low-level clouds are shown as yellow, high-level clouds as white. The pale yellow area at the top right is a large bank of sea fog.

EARTH AND SPACE | 11

Weather recording

Detailed information about the weather is collected at special weather stations on land and at sea, from weather balloons and from satellites which view the Earth from space. The information is recorded on weather maps called 'synoptic charts'. These are revised as new data comes in. Temperature, pressure, cloud cover, present weather, wind direction and wind speed are all recorded and plotted on to complex maps, which are analysed to forecast the coming weather conditions. Synoptic charts are the basis for all weather forecasts (Figure 3).

The daily recordings made at the weather stations include the maximum and minimum temperature, the amount of precipitation and the hours of sunshine.

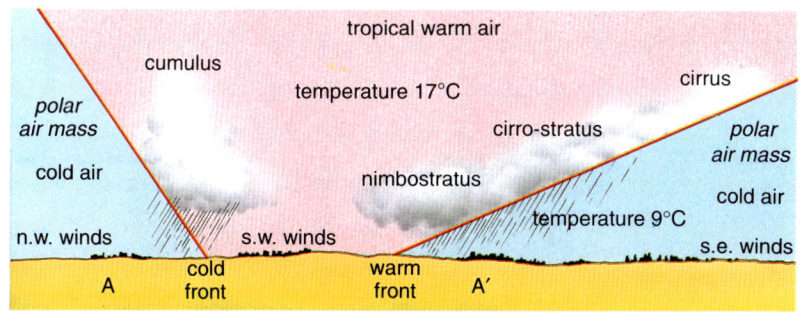

Figure 6
(a) Cross-section through a frontal system. Cold polar air pushes warm tropical air into an upwards spiral. Rain is heaviest at the cold front. The letters AA' connect this cross-section to Figure 5 (d)

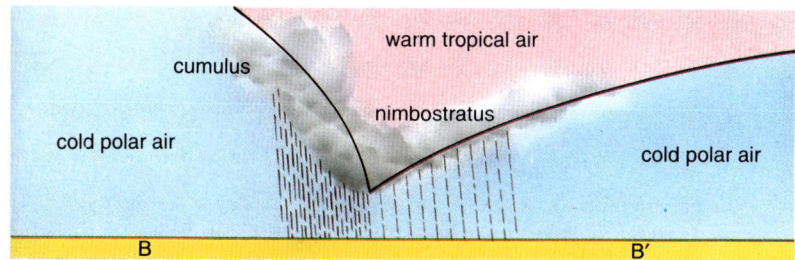

Figure 6
(b) This cross-section shows an occluded front. The warm tropical air has been lifted clear of the ground by the cold polar air masses. The letters BB' refer to Figure 5(d)

QUESTIONS

1 Explain what weather we should expect when the following air masses approach Britain: (i) polar maritime (ii) polar continental.

2 Explain the terms: warm front, cold front, occluded front.

3 (a) In the text it is stated that stronger wind blows where the pressure gradient is highest, explain why this is so.

(b) Explain what is meant by an isobar.

(c) Winds blow approximately along the lines of the isobars. Compare the directions and strengths of the wind at the points P and Q marked on the map in Figure 4.

4 The weather map shows a frontal system approaching Britain. Such a system might take 48 hours to pass over the country travelling west to east.

(a) Why do frontal systems arrive from the west?

(b) Imagine you are staying with a friend at point X on the map. Use the information in Figures 3 and 4 to describe how the weather changes over the period that the warm and then cold fronts pass over. In your answer you should mention: clouds, their height and type; the temperature; the wind direction and the rainfall.

(c) Look at the satellite photograph of the cold front. Describe carefully the atmospheric conditions immediately after the front has passed overhead.

5 WEATHERING, EROSION AND TRANSPORT

Our landscape is slowly and constantly changing. Several processes act upon it, wearing down old rocks and creating new ones. These processes involve **weathering**, **erosion**, **transport** and **deposition**. They have operated constantly since the Earth was first formed. They have lowered mountains to plains, creating sediments which may later be built up into mountains.

Weathering

The first stage in the cycle which wears down the landscape is **weathering**. Weathering involves the breakdown, fracturing and decomposition of rocks on or near the surface of the Earth. There are many different kinds of weathering. Some occur on a large scale, others at molecular level. They take place in normal atmospheric conditions and are helped along by changes in temperature and the presence of water.

Hard crystalline rocks are not necessarily more difficult to weather than the 'softer' sediments. Granite is very hard, yet one of its main components, feldspar, is particularly vulnerable to reaction with water (**hydrolysis**). In hydrolysis, the feldspar weathers to china clay (kaolin). On the other hand clay rocks are very soft, but they weather very little because clay minerals are the end product of weathering (they cannot be broken down further).

The main stages of weathering are shown in Figure 1.

Erosion

Erosion is different from weathering because it involves transport. **An agent of erosion** is something which can pick up particles and carry them along. So moving water in rivers and waves, winds (especially in deserts) and glaciers are the important agents of erosion. You can see examples of erosion in the photographs.

For wind and water, a critical speed of flow is needed before particles of a certain size can be picked up and carried along. If the speed of flow falls below this critical level, heavier particles will be deposited. The same is true for glaciers, like the one in the photograph, although the slow-moving ice of glaciers works on a totally different time scale from wind and rivers.

The rock particles carried in the agent wear away the landscape, like a scouring pad. Rivers wear away their channels, deepening and widening valleys. Coastal waves undercut cliffs and scrape out caves. Glaciers carve slowly and deeply like giant files. Desert winds sculpture and polish bare rock surfaces over wide areas. Little by little, these agents erode and alter the landscape.

Figure 1
Sequence of weathering processes

Water is an agent of erosion. Weathered material is transported by rivers to the sea where it is carried by water currents and wave action. The Scarisdale River, shown here, is able to transport fine material, as well as large boulders when it is in flood. The load it carries helps to erode its valley

Transport

Processes which operate in the transporting agents of water, wind and, to a much lesser degree, ice, have the effect of altering the shape and size of weathered particles which are picked up and carried. Freshly weathered rock particles are always angular but their sharp edges are gradually removed once they are picked up and transported. Particles carried by water or wind knock against each other, corners and sharp angles are broken off and the particles gradually become rounded. This is the process of **attrition**. **Abrasion** is the transport process where water and wind transported particles knock against the bedrock and erode it, gradually wearing away the landscape. This process of abrasion also helps to round the grains.

Particles which are transported by ice remain angular because, suspended in the ice, they cannot knock against each other. They may show smooth surfaces worn flat by abrasion if they have been carried near the glacier base or sides and have been scraped against the bedrock.

Deposition

When winds, rivers, waves and ice can no longer carry weathered material, it is deposited as sediment. With the transport agents of water and wind, the heaviest material is always deposited first and the lightest last. Down the course of a river, in shallow seas and in deserts particles are deposited in graduation from course gravels (the heaviest) to sands, silts and clays (the lightest). Water and wind deposit sorted sediments. When glaciers retreat or melt they deposit an unsorted load of all grain sizes from boulders to rock flour and there is no gradation in size.

Material transported by slow moving glaciers erodes the sides and floor of the valley

Sedimentation

Most sediment is deposited on the shallow continental shelves surrounding land masses. Here they form horizontal beds or strata. As the beds become buried under younger layers of sediment the weight of the overlying beds compacts the grains together and squeezes out water from between them. Mineral fluids fill in the small spaces between the grains and cements them together. The once soft, unconsolidated sediments are converted to hard sedimentary rocks.

Soil formation

Soils gradually form on weathered material, deposited sediment or bedrock which is exposed on the land surface. Weathering processes disintegrate and decompose the rock material creating a regolith or stony layer upon which plants can grow. Plants add organic matter to the immature soil which can then support animals. Gradually, over hundreds or even thousands of years, a mature soil develops consisting of about 45% mineral matter, 5% organic matter, and 25% water and 25% air. Poor soils tend to develop on sands and gravels, while we find better soils on silts and clays.

QUESTIONS

1 How does mechanical weathering make chemical weathering more effective?

2 Heat speeds up chemical reactions. So why does chemical weathering take place slowly in hot deserts?

3 Why is wind erosion relatively more important in arid (dry) regions of the world than in humid (wet) ones?

4 Describe two ways in which waves cause erosion. What typical landfoms of erosion are seen along the coastline?

The 'towers' in Monument Valley, Arizona, have been formed by the eroding action of the wind

6 THE ROCK CYCLE

*Figure 1
Formation of igneous, sedimentary and metamorphic rock*

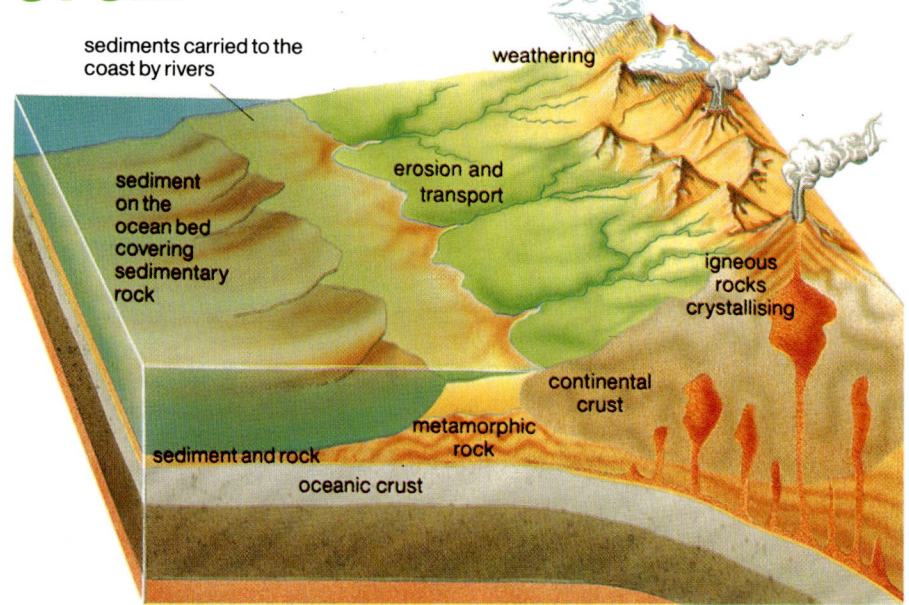

This is an example of an igneous rock. 'Igneous' means 'formed by fire' because these rocks result from the cooling of molten magma on, or within, the Earth. The size of the crystals depend on how quickly the magma cools. This rock has cooled slowly so its crystals are large.

When the Earth first cooled, its molten crust solidified to form **igneous rock**. Igneous means 'formed by fire'. Initially there was no other type of rock. Over thousands and millions of years, two other types of rock were created. These were **sedimentary rocks** and **metamorphic rocks**. Figure 1 shows how these three types of rock are forming today.

Igneous rocks

Igneous rocks originate from the liquid rock, or magma, below the Earth's crust. **Lava** from volcanoes is magma pouring out from cracks in the Earth's crust. When magma or lava cools and crystallises, igneous rock is formed (Figure 1). The size of crystals in the igneous rock depends on the rate of cooling. Lava loses its heat very rapidly to the air, so above the Earth's surface it quickly becomes a solid. The lava crystallises in days or months depending on its thickness. This process produces rocks, such as **basalt**, with small crystals. Magma which is cooling *below* the Earth's surface retains its heat far longer. It may not cool to a solid for centuries so the crystals have a very long time in which to grow. This produces rocks like **granite** with large coarse-grained crystals.

Sedimentary rocks

This is an example of a sedimentary rock, formed from the breakdown products of older rocks

When igneous rocks are exposed at the surface of the Earth, they undergo weathering and erosion. These processes form sediments which are carried from their original location and deposited elsewhere. Most sediment is deposited on the shallow **continental shelves** surrounding land masses (Figure 1). As the weathered material is brought down from the eroding land masses, successive beds, or **strata** form. In some areas, chalk sediments have formed from the calcium carbonate present in the shells of sea animals. As the beds become buried deeper, they are compacted under the weight of the layers above. This converts the soft sediments to harder sedimentary limestone rocks.

Metamorphic rocks

In some cases, sedimentary rock has been buried to great depths and been changed by enormous pressure and high temperatures. This has produced **metamorphic rocks** (Figure 1). There are various types of metamorphic rock depending upon the type of sediment from which they originate. The minerals in the parent sediment are sometimes changed under the stresses of heat and pressure. In some cases, they are changed to chemically similar, but harder and more stable metamorphic rocks. This results in a series of physically different metamorphic rocks. Deep down inside the Earth, the base of the metamorphic rock may melt, creating magma. This will eventually solidify as igneous rock, beginning the rock cycle again.

Figure 2 shows the various stages of the rock cycle. The complete rock cycle, lasting hundreds of millions of years, does not always take place exactly as described. Sometimes, igneous rock, instead of weathering at the surface, may be subjected to heat and pressure and become metamorphic rock. Metamorphic and sedimentary rocks may also weather and erode to form new sedimentary rocks. Not all old rocks are turned into sediment and recycled. Some of them have been covered and protected by successive layers of younger rocks since the Earth was first formed 4600 million years ago.

This is an example of a metamorphic rock, formed from sedimentary rock under high temperature and pressure. The minerals in metamorphic rocks can help geologists to trace their origin

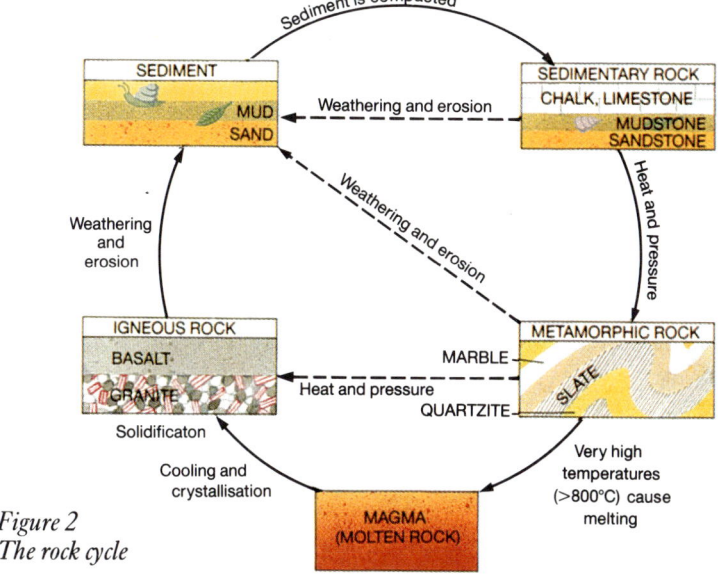

*Figure 2
The rock cycle*

QUESTIONS

1 Using the rock cycle in Figure 2, explain the following statement: 'one rock is the raw material for another'.

2 When the Earth first formed, there were only igneous rocks.
(a) Why was this?
(b) How did sedimentary and metamorphic rocks come into existence?

3 (a) Describe how sediments may form on land and in the sea.
(b) How are they turned into sedimentary rocks?

4 You are given three pieces of rock by a friend who wants to know more about them.

Rock A is made of rounded pebbles held together by a hard, sandy layer.

Rock B is white in colour and contains several small fossils which look like shells you have seen at the seaside.

Rock C is very hard and is made of large crystals which you can see quite clearly.

What could you tell your friend about the rocks?

7 THE STRUCTURE OF THE EARTH

Internal structure of the Earth

The Earth is shaped like an orange, spherical but slightly flattened at the poles. Its structure and surface is like a badly cracked egg. The 'cracked shell' is the very thin **crust**, the 'white' is the **mantle** and the 'yolk' is the **core** (Figure 1). These concentric layers increase in thickness, density and temperature towards the centre. Evidence for the Earth's structure comes from various sources. Information about the crust comes from studying mines, volcanoes and earthquakes. Evidence for the mantle and the core comes from the study of earthquakes, deep volcanoes, meteorites and the Earth's magnetic field.

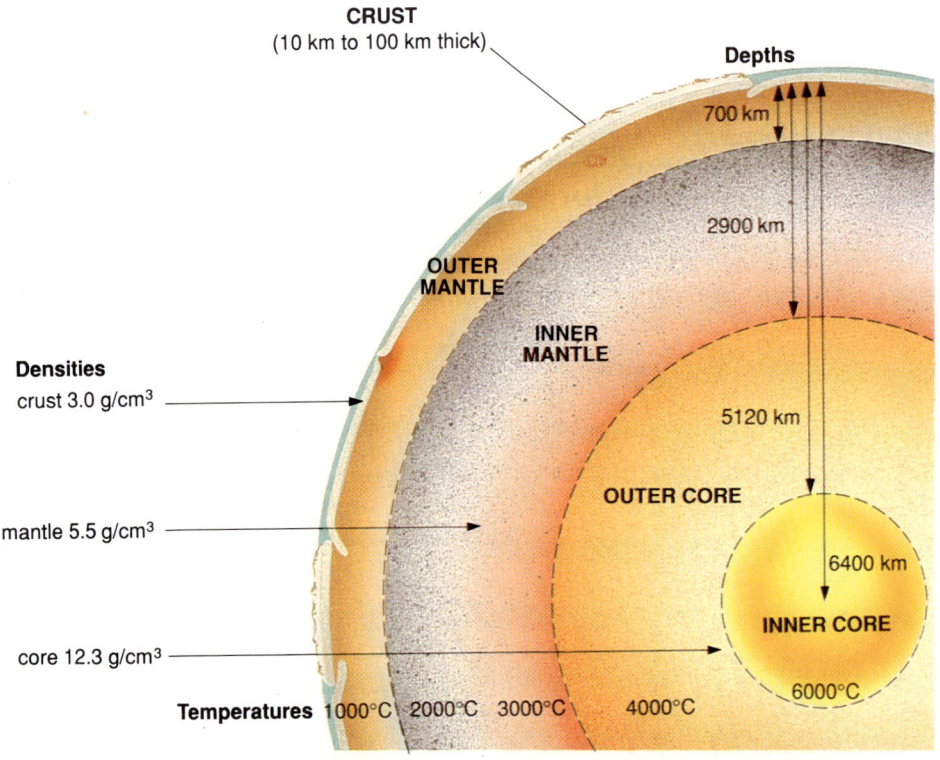

Figure 1
Cross-section of the Earth to show its internal structure

Figure 1 shows a cross-section of the Earth. The Earth's crust is composed of igneous, metamorphic and sedimentary rocks. The crust is very thin and is broken into large and small parts, called **plates**. These float on the denser mantle, parts of which are molten. Over long periods of geological time, changes occur in the crust. Immense internal forces cause the plates to move resulting in faults, rift valleys, volcanoes and earthquakes. In some parts, the crust is being stretched and is under tension. Deep cracks appear in the crust, rocks break and one side slips down filling the space created. This forms a **fault**. **Rift valleys** form where two normal faults lie alongside each other (Figure 2). Deep cracks in the Earth's surface can also lead to volcanoes. In other parts of the Earth, the crust is being pushed together and compressed (Figure 2(b) and 2(c)). This causes layers of the crust to ride over each other and fold, resulting in earthquakes (Figure 2(d)).

The mantle and the core are so deep in the Earth that they are normally inaccessible but, in The Lizard in Cornwall, mantle rock has been pushed to the surface and can be seen. Mantle rocks can also be studied from **xenoliths** ('strange rocks') brought up in volcanoes.

Evidence for the Earth's structure

Much greater detail of the Earth's structure comes from the study of earthquakes and magnetic fields. During an earthquake, the crust ruptures. Energy generated at the focus of the earthquake creates a train of shock (**seismic**) waves. These extend outwards through the Earth and their pathways are shown in Figure 3. Earthquake energy creates three main types of waves: **P** or **primary waves**; **S, secondary** or **shear waves**; **L, longitudinal or surface waves**. L waves are slow moving and travel through the crust. P and S waves move faster and travel through the deeper layers of the Earth (Figure 3). P waves travel at 5 km per second and pass through liquids and solids. S waves travel at 3 km per second and only pass through solids. They cannot pass through the Earth's liquid outer core. From the movement of these waves we can obtain evidence for the Earth's internal structure. Surface waves roll invisibly through the Earth's crust. Around the **epicentre** of an earthquake (right above the focus) these waves cause the most damage to buildings.

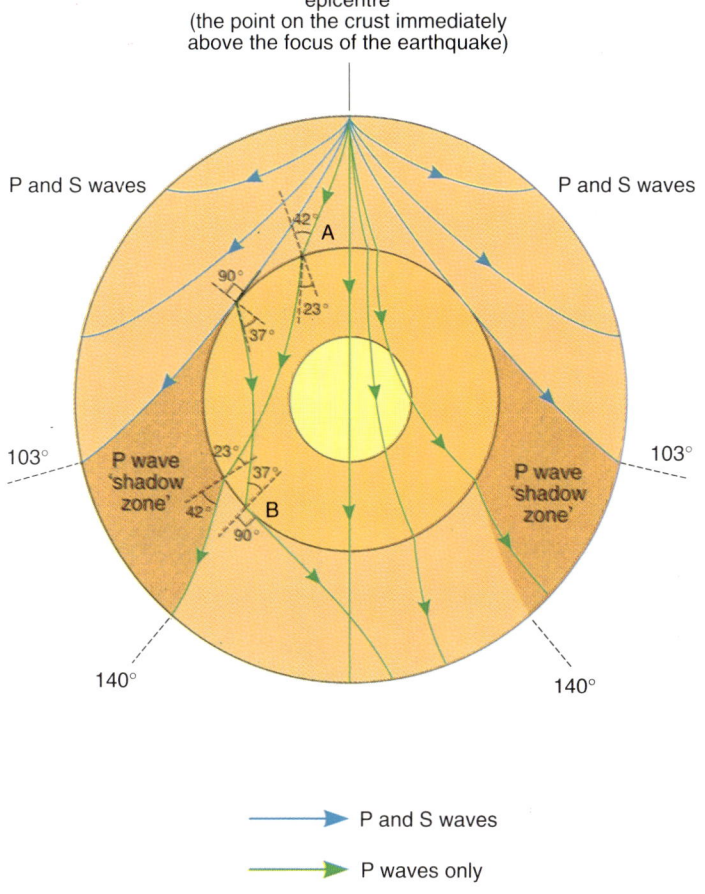

Figure 3
Cross-section of the Earth showing the paths of seismic waves from an earthquake. Both P and S waves spread out to angles up to 103° from the epicentre, but S waves cannot travel through the liquid core. P waves entering the liquid core slow down and are focused (like light waves through a lens) into the region at the bottom of the diagram (angles >140°). No P wave travelling through the liquid outer core reaches the 'P wave shadow zone'. However, weak P waves are detected in that zone, which have been speeded up, and therefore refracted, by the solid inner core

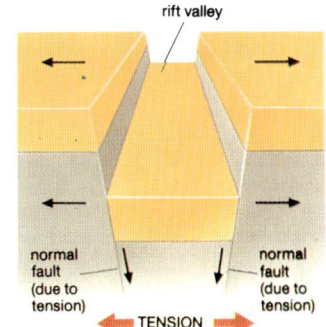

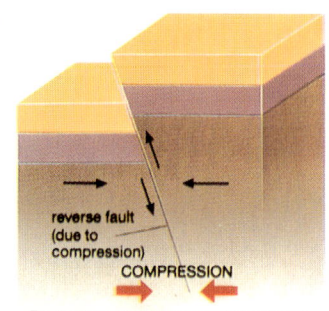

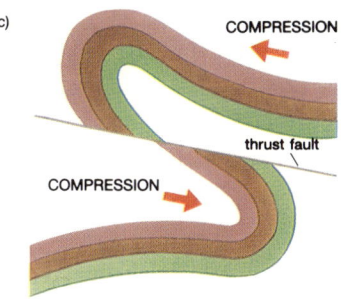

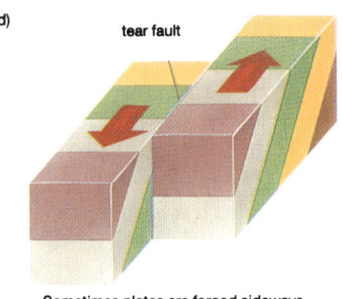

Figure 2
(a) Normal faults and a rift-valley
(b) Reverse fault
(c) Thrust fault   (d) Tear fault

18 THE STRUCTURE OF THE EARTH

S waves do not register on earthquake recording equipment at an angle greater than 105° from the **epicentre** of the earthquake. P waves are also cut out after 105° but reappear again at 140° from the epicentre. Between 105° and 140°, a **shadow zone** exists where no earthquake information can be traced. This suggests that S waves cannot pass through the liquid outer core. P waves, are, however, refracted through the core, reappearing at 140°.

Seismic waves

Seismic wave velocity depends on the density and elasticity of the rock it is passing through. Rigid, crystalline rock transmits waves faster than unconsolidated sediments because it can elastically spring back once waves have passed through.

The speed of seismic waves generally increases with depth because, under greater pressure, the rock is more compact and elastic.

Longitudinal P waves oscillate in the same direction as the direction of their motion like sound waves, causing elastic rock material to alternately compress and then expand. Both liquids and solids respond elastically. Sheer S waves oscillate at right angles to their direction of motion. They cannot travel through liquids because liquids do not resist changes in shape. Instead they simply flow. Whatever the material, P waves always travel faster than S waves.

Figure 4 Variation in P and S waves with depth

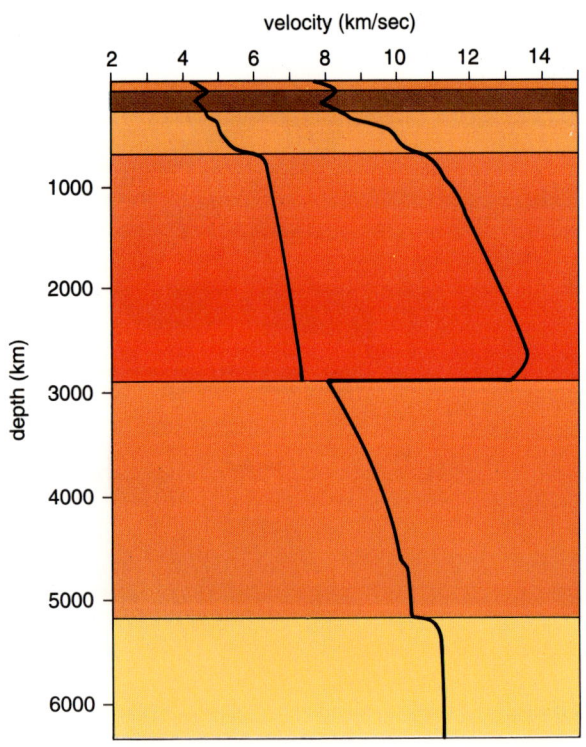
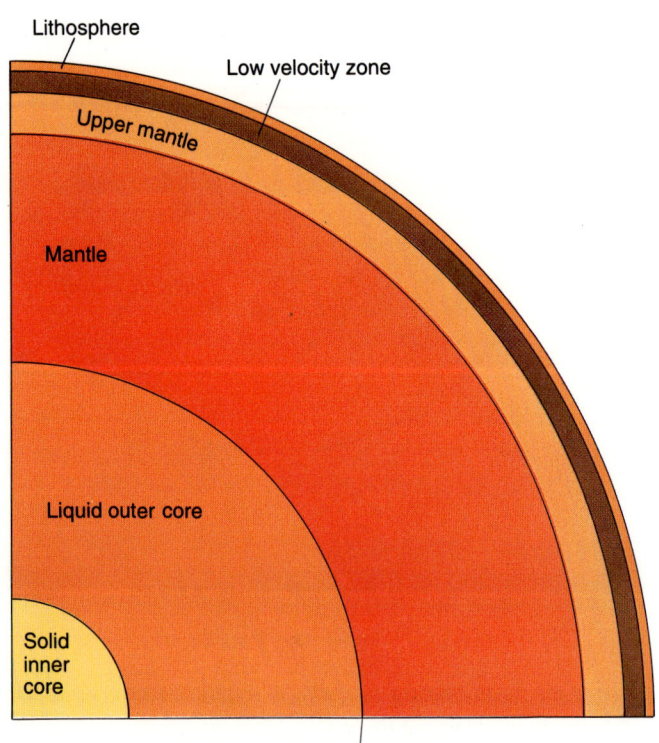

Seismic waves are bent or refracted when they pass from one material to another (provided they are not travelling at right angles to the boundary). Some energy is either reflected back from the boundary, or **discontinuity**. Abrupt changes occur at particular depths worldwide due to material of different densities sorting into layers that took place as the Earth formed. Other, more localised, changes occur where rock has either partially melted or has a different crystalline structure.

Sudden variations in the speed of P and S waves have shown geophysicists the major layers and features of the Earth's interior and the depths at which they occur.

The Earth's magnetic field

The Earth has a strong magnetic field which is produced as the Earth spins on its axis. The fluid outer core allows the mantle and the crust to rotate faster than the solid inner core. This produces a magnetic field similar to an enormous bar magnet (Figure 6). The magnetism exists because the Earth has an iron-rich core. Rocks in the Earth's crust which contain iron also take on this magnetism as they solidify. Magnetic particles in the crust show that the crust must have moved over geological time.

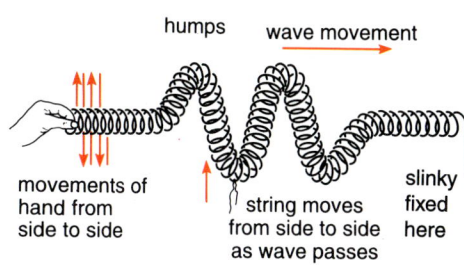

Figure 5
(a) S waves are transverse waves. The rock oscillates at right angles to the direction of the wave movement. S waves can only travel through solids.

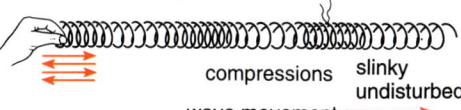

(b) P waves are longitudinal waves. They are rather like a series of compressions and expansions passing along a slinky. Longitudinal waves can pass through solids, liquids and gases.

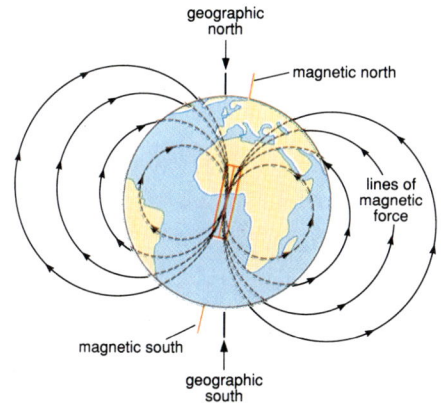

Figure 6
The Earth's magnetic field

QUESTIONS

1 In California, you can see orange groves with trees growing in perfect, straight lines. However, there are some orange groves in which the lines of trees are for some reason kinked. They were not planted like that.
(a) What is the cause?
(b) In what interesting geological area are these orange groves?

2 The crust of the Earth is thought to account for only 1% of the total volume of the Earth. The mantle accounts for about 82%. Using these figures, construct a pie chart for the major layers of the Earth.

3 Although some very deep holes have been drilled into the Earth, none has ever reached the mantle. We have no direct evidence of the nature of the interior of the Earth. Our knowledge is based on indirect evidence. What is this evidence and what has it told us about the Earth's interior?

4 Imagine that a major earthquake happens somewhere in the British Isles. Seismological (earthquake) stations in Paris, New York, Peking and Nairobi all know that an earthquake has occurred. In Auckland, where they often monitor major earthquakes, only weak P waves are detected. Explain this.

5 This question is about the path of seismic waves through the Earth in Figure 3.
(a) When P waves enter the core at point A they are refracted towards the normal. Use Figure 4 to explain the direction of their refraction. (Hint: what happens when light travels from air to glass?)
(b) As the P waves pass from A to B their path curves continuously towards the surface. Use Figure 4 to explain this curvature.

8 PLATE TECTONICS

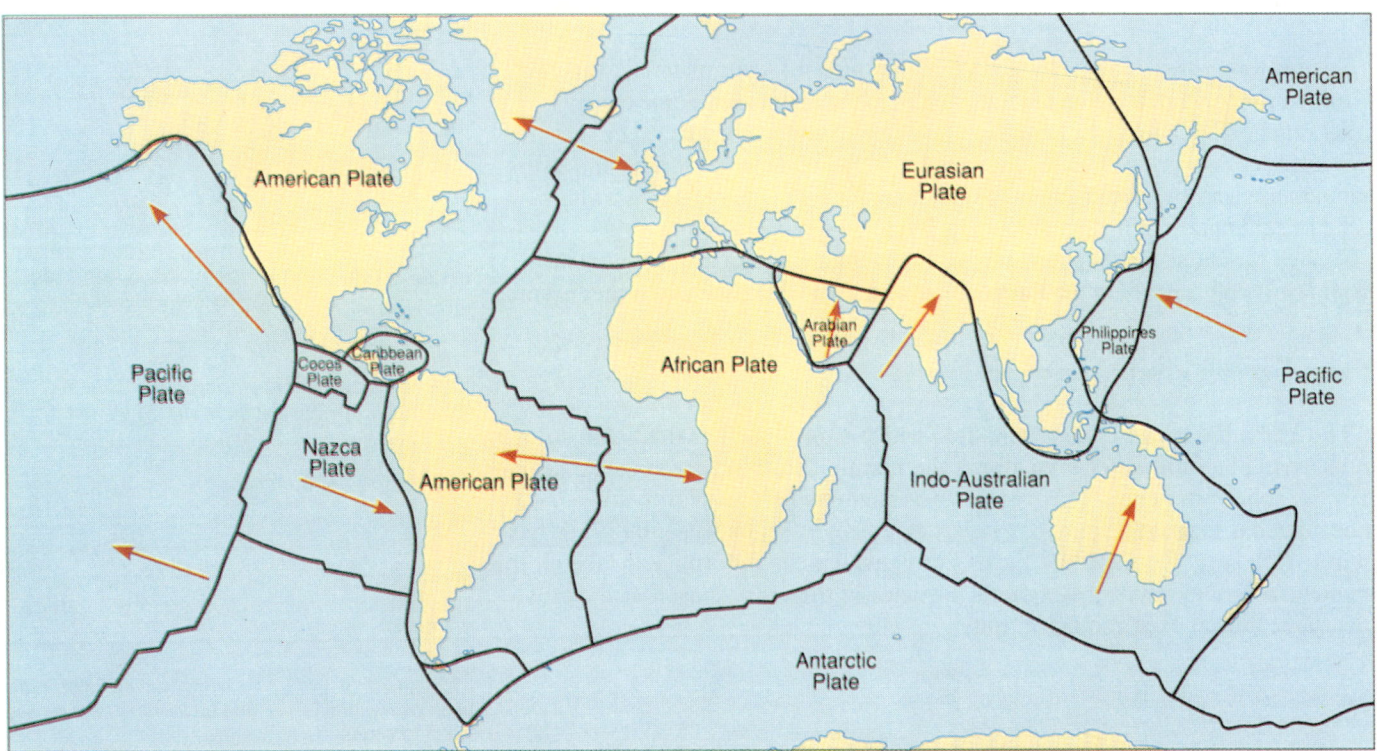

Figure 1
World map showing the main plates and their directions of movement

The structure and physical properties of the Earth are the key to understanding **plate tectonics**. The Earth's core is as hot as the surface of the Sun. This causes slow convection currents in the liquid mantle which result in slow movements in the plates of the Earth's crust. This is the start of the **tectonic cycle**. Figure 1 shows how these plates are moving.

Many years ago, Africa and Arabia used to be joined together. They are now growing apart as the Red Sea gradually widens. This sea may eventually become as large as the Atlantic Ocean

EARTH AND SPACE **21**

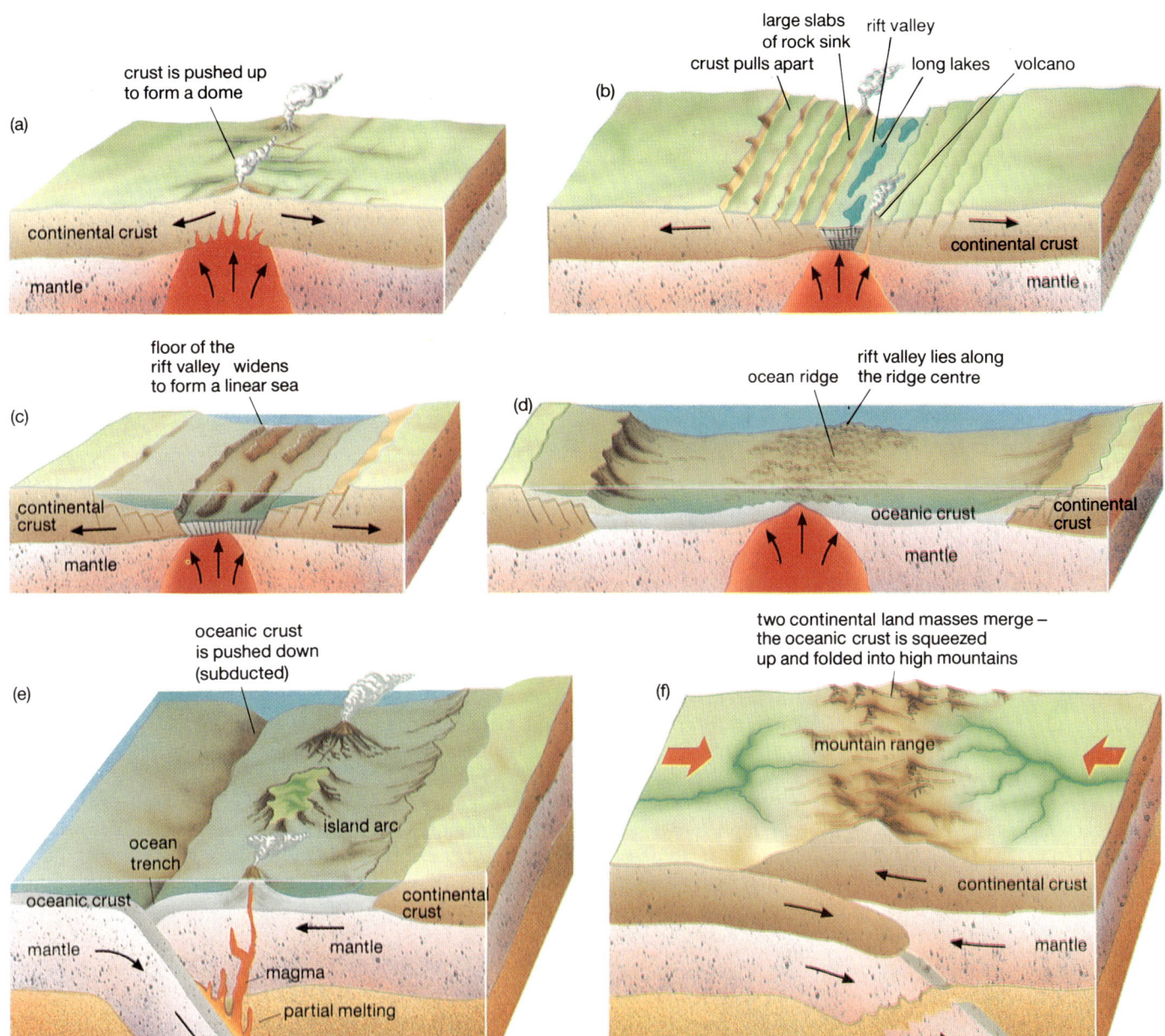

The convection currents circulating in the liquid mantle may take millions of years to rise to the surface. If currents of hot, molten rock rise under the thin oceanic crust they form '**hot spots**' of intense volcanic activity. The Hawaiian islands lie above one of these hot spots. On these islands, magma rises to the crust surface forming '**shield volcanoes**'; the 'runny' basalt lava flows quickly so shield volcanoes have gentle slopes. Under the thicker continental crust, rising convection currents push the crust up into a dome, causing tension and cracking (Figure 2(a)). As the crust is pulled apart, large slabs of rock sink and rift valleys form. Volcanoes appear where the magma escapes from cracks in the rift valley (Figure 2(b)). This is typical of the rift valleys in East Africa.

The Red Sea and Gulf of Aden illustrate the next stage of the tectonic cycle when the floor of the rift valley can widen to form a **linear sea** (Figure 2(c)).

Figure 2
(a) The continental crust is pushed up into a dome
(b) Rift valleys form with volcanoes
(c) A linear sea develops
(d) An ocean ridge forms and the ocean widens
(e) An ocean trench forms with island arcs; the oceanic crust is subducted (pushed down)
(f) As continents collide, the ocean closes and a larger land mass with high mountains is formed

PLATE TECTONICS

This region will gradually form a new ocean, separating Africa from Arabia. The Atlantic is an example of an expanding young ocean. It is widening as fast as your fingernails grow. A submerged ocean ridge has formed down the centre of the Atlantic from the Arctic to the Antarctic (Figure 2(d)). This **mid-Atlantic ridge** follows the boundary between the American Plate and the African and Eurasian Plates (Figure 1). A rift valley lying along the centre of the ridge, slowly generates new oceanic floor. So the mid-Atlantic ridge is called a **constructive plate margin**.

As the Atlantic Ocean widens, the Pacific Ocean is slowly closing. The Pacific is a much older ocean than the Atlantic. Over millions and millions of years, thick deposits of sediment have collected on the ocean floor. The layers of sediment are particularly thick near continents where rivers have carried silt into the ocean. As the oceanic crust is thin, the weight of sediment makes it sag. More sediment collects, and eventually the crust breaks. As new crust is being created at the ocean ridge, the old oceanic crust, near to the continent, is pushed down or **subducted** (Figure 2(e)).

The deep depression in the crust where subduction occurs is called an **ocean trench**. Subduction of the ocean crust and wet sediment into the mantle creates magma which rises up to the surface. Some escapes as thick, explosive lava, forming volcanic islands in arcs which fringe the trench (Figure 2(e)). There are island arcs which extend from the Aleutian Trench in the north-west Pacific to the Tonga Trench in the south-west Pacific. Some islands form larger island groups like Japan. Ocean trenches are part of a **destructive plate margin**, because ocean floor disappears into them.

As the Atlantic grows, the American continents are moving westwards. Along the western edge of South America, the Nazca Plate is being pushed against the American Plate (Figure 1). Here the ocean crust is being forced under the advancing landmass. This is pushing up marine sediments and creating the Andes Mountains. In California, the North American Plate and the Pacific Plate are moving sideways past each other along the San Andreas Fault. No land is being formed or destroyed along this fault, so we call it a **conservative plate margin**.

A tectonic cycle ends when two continental land masses converge and the ocean between them disappears. The layers of oceanic crust are squeezed into tight folds forming high mountains (Figure 2(f)). This is what happened when India moved north to collide with Asia. The ancient Tethys Ocean disappeared and the Himalayan mountains were formed. The crust here is so thick that volcanic activity has stopped, although earthquakes are common.

If the Earth was filmed from outer space using time lapse photography over a period of 1000 million years, you would be able to see the tectonic cycle clearly: continents moving apart, oceans waxing and waning, new continents joining and mountain chains forming.

These mountains were formed from horizontal beds of sediment at the bottom of an ancient ocean. As the continents moved together and the ocean closed up, this sediment was pushed up into a fold mountain range

QUESTIONS

1 Using an atlas, find named examples of volcanoes for each of the following stages in the tectonic cycle (the areas in brackets will help you):
(a) continental rifting (East African Rift valley),
(b) linear sea spreading (Red Sea and Gulf of Aden),
(c) growth of ocean (islands on the Atlantic ridge),
(d) subduction of ocean floor far from continents, (island arcs near deep trenches),
(e) subduction of ocean floor near to continents (the Andes and the Rockies).

Are there any volcanoes in the final stage of the cycle, (e.g. the Himalayas)? Are there any other locations where volcanoes can be found? If so, why are they found there?

2 What do we mean by the 'jig-saw fit' of continents?

9 EVIDENCE FOR PLATE TECTONICS

A wealth of evidence today supports the theory put forward by Alfred Wegener in 1915, that continents are not fixed in their position but have in fact drifted apart over geological time.

Continents can be 'fitted' together along their shelf margins like pieces of a jigsaw puzzle, with very little mismatch. Africa and South America illustrate this very well. Not only do they fit together well but the 'jigsaw picture' matches in terms of specific rock types and fossils found on either side (Figure 1(a)).

Mesozoic fossils common to both Africa and South America are separated by the wide South Atlantic Ocean. *Mesosaurus* (Figure 1b), a small swimming reptile, not capable of swimming the Atlantic, is a fossil found on both continents. The Atlantic ocean opened at the end of the Mesozoic era separating Africa and South America and later Cenozoic placental mammals, largely unique to each continent, evolved. Where continental separation was complete, as in Australia which drifted from South America and Antarctica, egg laying and marsupial mammals evolved in isolation.

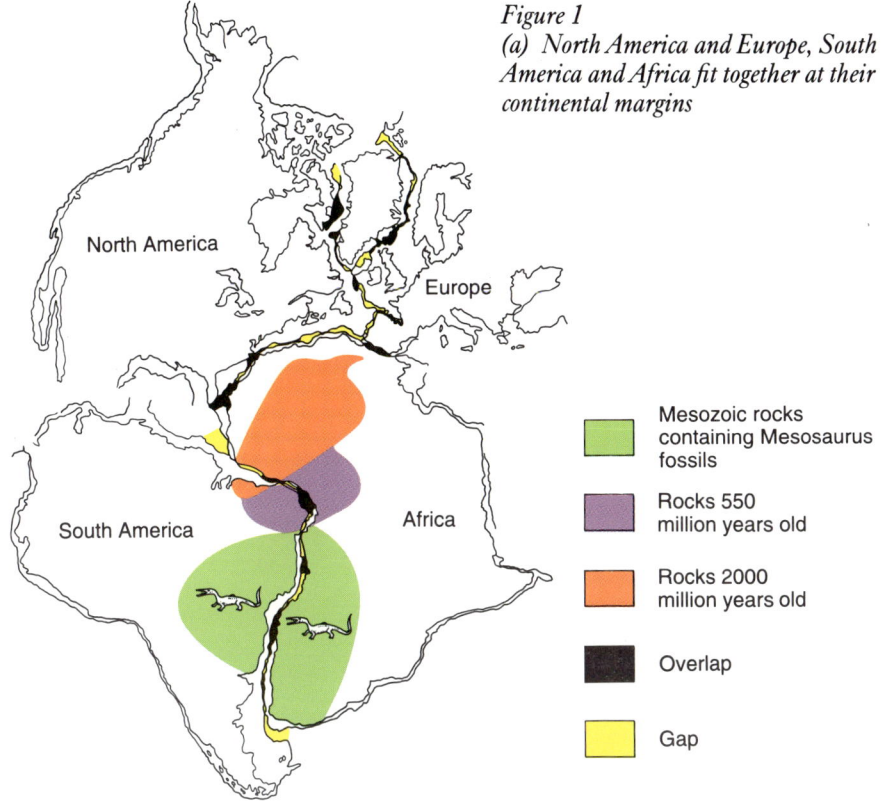

Figure 1
(a) North America and Europe, South America and Africa fit together at their continental margins

(b) Mesosaurus

Mountain chains can be traced from one continent to another, for example the mountains of Norway and Scotland fit perfectly with those of Greenland and North America. They were once one long chain that the North Atlantic now separates.

Today coral reefs only grow in warm tropical seas and coal can only be formed in equatorial swamp conditions, yet fossil coral reefs and thick coal seams are found in Britain and Northern Europe. Likewise, ancient desert sandstones can be seen in Scotland and glacial sediments occur in South Africa neither of which have appropriate climatic conditions for their formation today. This **palaeoclimatic** evidence from specific rock types proves that continents have drifted very slowly over time (Figure 2).

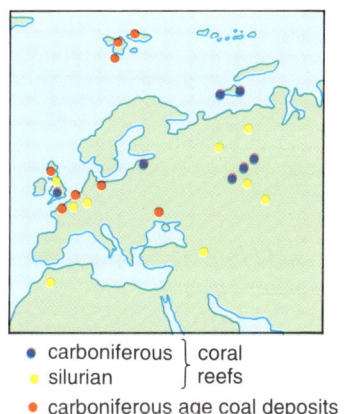

Figure 2
Map of North America and Europe showing ancient coral reefs and Carboniferous age coal deposits

EVIDENCE FOR PLATE TECTONICS

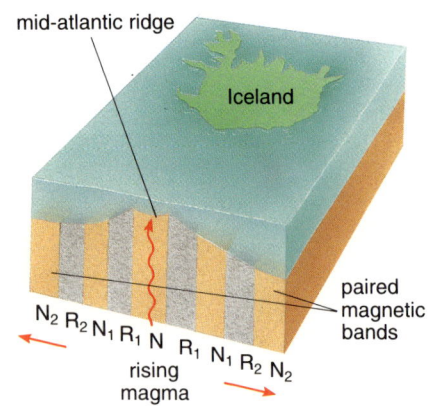

Figure 3
Earth's magnetic reversals and banding

Certain rocks, particularly basalt, contain iron-rich minerals. When these rocks formed, the iron-rich minerals became magnetised in the same direction as the Earth's magnetic field, taking on a 'fossil' magnetism or **palaeomagnetism**. These rocks not only show the direction of the pole when they formed but, from their orientation, the latitude as well. In the 1950s, maps drawn to show the position of magnetic north through time appeared to show that it had gradually moved. This phenomenon was called **polar wander**. Today we know that the north pole has not moved but it is the continents which have.

The Earth's magnetism also helped prove that the ocean floor is growing at the mid-oceanic ridges. The fact that oceans are relatively young and impermanent, growing at ocean ridges and being destroyed in ocean trenches, is the mechanism whereby continents slowly move (and eventually collide). Basalt extruded on the ridges as continents move apart takes on the Earth's magnetism. It is known that the Earth's magnetic pole changes from north to south over geological time. This is called **magnetic reversal**. Basalt solidifying on ocean ridges today shows normal polarity but on either side, the sea floor shows reverse polarity. Equal strips of magnetic banding, normal and reverse, are found on each side (Figure 3). Studies of magnetic banding have helped determine spreading rates. The North Atlantic is spreading 1–2cm (each side) and the South Pacific 3–10cm (each side) per year.

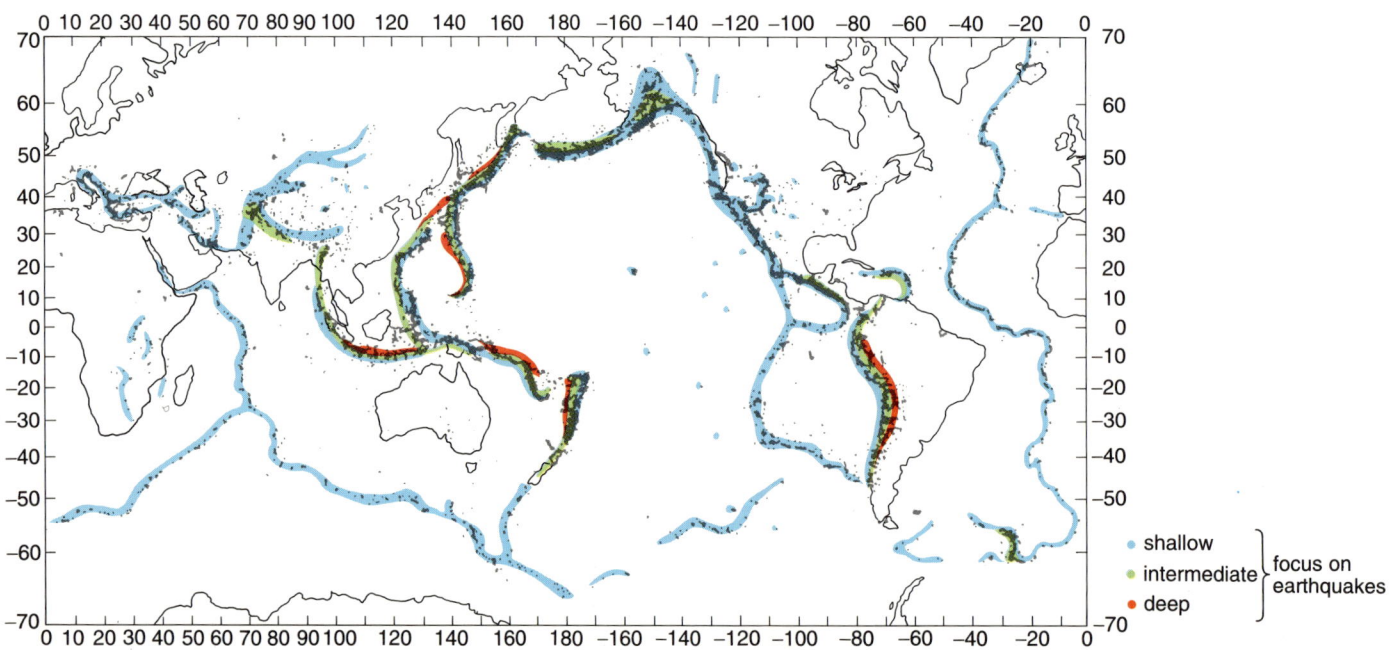

Figure 4
Map of the world showing seismically active zones at all plate boundaries

Earthquake studies of the Earth's seismically active zones show that shallow foci earthquakes correspond with ocean ridges – **constructive** plate margins. Shallow, intermediate and deep foci earthquakes correspond with ocean trenches – **destructive** plate margins (Figure 4). The active San Andreas fault marks the conservative plate margin of the North American Plate.

The latest evidence supporting the theory of plate tectonics comes from space technology. Lasers mounted on satellites orbiting the Earth are today measuring oceanic growth as little as 1–2cm per year.

Evidence for Britain's northward drift is shown in Silurian coral limestones, Devonian desert sandstones, Carboniferous limestones and coal, Permian desert sandstones, and Jurassic coral limestones.

EARTH AND SPACE

Geological eras	Geological periods	Synopsis of Britain's northerly drift since Cambrian times
Cenozoic	Holocene / Pleistocene — 1.8	Britain lies in temperate latitudes, moving slower eastwards as the Atlantic ocean expands.
Cenozoic (tertiary)	Pliocene / Miocene / Oligocene	Movement of African plate northwards closes an ocean and pushes up the Alps and forms the hills of Southern England.
Cenozoic (tertiary)	Eocene / Palaeocene — 65	The opening and growth of the North Atlantic. Eurasian and North American plates separate. Volcanic activity at constructive margin.
Mesozoic	Cretaceous — 140	Tropical warm seas. Chalk formed.
Mesozoic	Jurassic — 195	Tropical warm seas. Corals and oolithic limestones formed in shallow, warm, clear seas.
Mesozoic	Triassic — 230	Hot, dry desert conditions. Salt lakes, shallow salty seas. Desert sandstones.
		Formation of Pangaea
Palaeozoic (upper)	Permian — 280	Ocean closure and the collision of continents. Desert sandstones formed in northern desert latitudes.
Palaeozoic (upper)	upper Carboniferous / lower — 345	Coral reef limestones formed in tropical latitudes and coal formed in Equatorial latitudes as the plates drifted further north.
Palaeozoic (upper)	Devonian — 395	Caledonian mountains built as the plates collided. The linked plates drifted north through southern desert latitudes.
Palaeozoic (lower)	Silurian — 435	Coral reefs formed in the tropical latitudes of the waining ocean.
Palaeozoic (lower)	Ordovician — 500	Volcanic activity as the ocean separating these two plates gradually closed.
Palaeozoic (lower)	Cambrian — 570	Northern Scotland lay on the American plate. England and Wales on the Eurasian plate.

Britain's latitude (but not longitude) — showing present shape and position at 60°N, and earlier positions through 30°N, 0°, and 30°S.

N.B. Britain did not have its present day shape in the past.

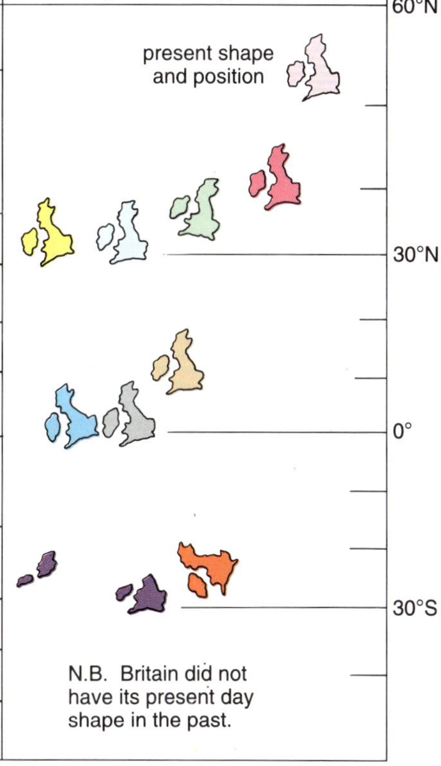

Figure 5 Britain's northward drift over time

QUESTIONS

1 The students in the photograph are drawing a field sketch of the fold.
(a) If the camera was facing east, which directions do you think the forces which created the fold came from?
(b) Was the force one of compression or tension? Draw a simple sketch of the fold and label the following: beds, upfold, downfold, direction of force, type of force.

2 Make a large copy of the map of the Hawaiian islands shown. Label each island with the age data given below and then answer the questions.
Hawaii – Less than 1 million years old.
Kauai – 5.6 to 3.8 million years old.
Maui – (north west) 1.3 to 1.15 million years old.
Maui – (south east) 0.8 million years old.
Molokai – 1.8 to 1.3 million years old.
Oahu – 3.4 to 2.2 million years old.

As continents gradually move together and the oceans between them become smaller, the rocks of the Earth's crust on the ocean bed are pushed up into folds. These small folds at Lulworth in Dorset are an example

(a) What is the age difference between the oldest and the youngest Hawaiian island?
(b) Label the oldest island 'not volcanically active', and the youngest 'volcanically active'.
(c) What are the compass bearings for the direction of movement of the Pacific plate? Draw an arrow to represent this on to your map.
(d) By accurately measuring the distance between the oldest and youngest islands, calculate the rate of movement of the Pacific plate in this area.

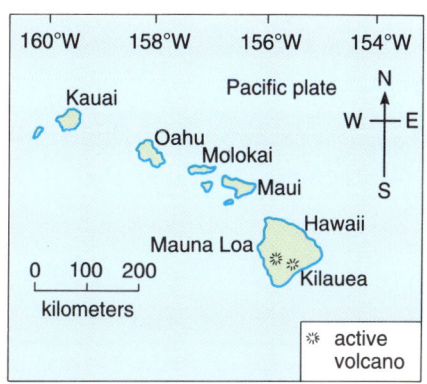

10 THE SOLAR SYSTEM

The brightest thing that you can see in the sky is our **Sun**. The Sun is a **star**, which provides all the heat and light that we need to live. The Earth is a **planet** which moves around the Sun. Altogether, there are nine planets which move round the Sun in curved paths. These paths are called **orbits**. The Earth is the third planet out from the Sun. Planets do not produce their own light like the Sun; we can see planets at night because they *reflect* the Sun's light. The Sun and its nine planets are known as the **solar system**. The word 'solar' means 'belonging to the sun'. Some of the planets have **moons** that move around them. The Earth has only one moon.

The four planets nearest to the Sun, including the Earth, have hard, solid and rocky surfaces. The planet closest to the sun is **Mercury**. This has a cratered surface that looks like our Moon's surface. During the day, Mercury is baking hot. Even lead would melt on its surface. Mercury travels quickly round the Sun, taking 88 days to complete one orbit.

Venus lies between Mercury and the Earth. It has a thick atmosphere; its clouds are made from burning hot sulphuric acid. Nothing could survive on its hot, poisonous surface.

Mars is the last of the rocky planets. It is a lot colder than the Earth because it is further away from the Sun. Like the Earth, it has large polar icecaps, which can be seen through a telescope. At some stage in the past, Mars had active volcanoes. The largest is called Olympus Mons. It towers 25 km above the surrounding land, this is more than 2½ times the height of Mount Everest above sea level. As continents move on the Earth, mountains grow. The Himalayas are growing now at about the same rate as your fingernails. Mountains may still be growing on Mars.

Beyond the orbit of Mars, are four giant planets: **Jupiter**, **Saturn**, **Uranus** and **Neptune**. Each of these is much larger than the four inner planets (Figure 1). In Figure 2, you can see that these four giant planets move in orbits that are far away from the Sun. Each of these planets is made from gas. If you landed on one of these planets, you would sink into it.

Illustration of the planet Mars to show the large polar ice cap. A system of canyons can be seen at the equator. At the top left of the picture you can see the Olympus Mons volcano, with three smaller volcanoes below it

Figure 1
The relative sizes of the Sun and its planets. (Figure 2 shows the positions of the planets relative to one another)

The largest planet is Jupiter, which has a diameter 11 times bigger than that of the Earth. More than 1000 Earths would be needed to fill Jupiter's enormous volume. The swirling clouds in Jupiter's atmosphere blow around at hurricane wind speeds of 200 miles per hour. Jupiter has 14 moons which orbit around it. Four of these are about the same size as our Moon. The innermost of these four large moons is called Io; when Voyager 1 flew by Io in 1979, it photographed active volcanoes. Saturn is best known for its beautiful rings.

EARTH AND SPACE 27

The planet furthest from the Sun is Pluto; it is smaller than our Moon. It is a frozen and dead world. Its temperature is 240 degrees below freezing. From its cold surface, the Sun would look like a bright star, not the provider of life giving light and warmth that we know.

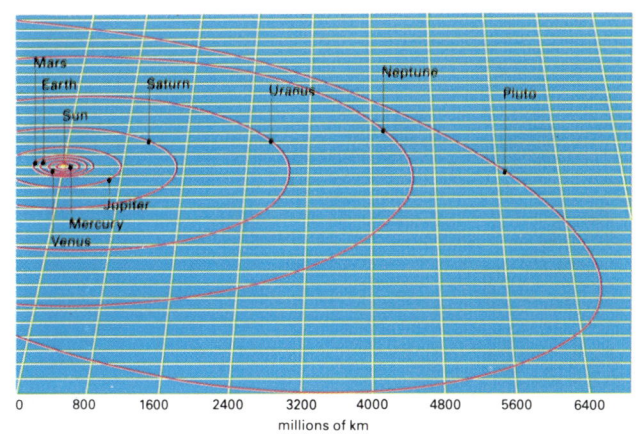

Figure 2
The orbits of the planets around the Sun. The four inner planets are very close to the Sun; the gaps between the outer planets are very large

Facts about the planets

Planet	Diameter of planet	Average distance of planet from the Sun	Time taken to go round the Sun	Number of moons	Average temperature on sunny side
Mercury	4900 km	58 million km	88 days	0	350°C
Venus	12 000 km	108 million km	225 days	0	480°C
Earth	12 800 km	150 million km	365¼ days	1	20°C
Mars	6800 km	228 million km	687 days	2	0°C
Jupiter	143 000 km	780 million km	12 years	14	−150°C
Saturn	120 000 km	1430 million km	29 years	24	−190°C
Uranus	52 000 km	2800 million km	84 years	15	−220°C
Neptune	49 000 km	4500 million km	165 years	3	−240°C
Pluto	3000 km	5900 million km	248 years	1	−240°C

Table 1

Facts about the Sun: diameter 1 400 000 km; surface temperature 6000°C.

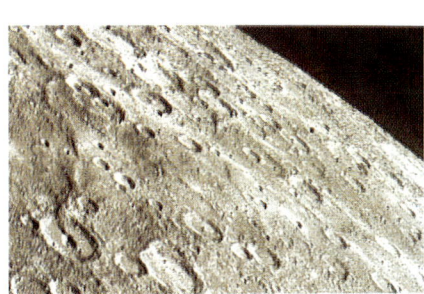

Mercury is only 58 million km from the Sun. It has a hot surface with no atmosphere to protect it from meteors. This photograph shows how the surface has been heavily cratered by meteors

QUESTIONS

1 Use Table 1 to help you answer these questions.
(a) Which is the largest planet?
(b) Which planet has a temperature closest to that of our Earth?
(c) Which planet takes just under two years to go round the Sun?
(d) Are the temperatures of the planets related to their distance from the Sun? Why is Venus hotter than Mercury?
(e) Is there any pattern in the number of moons that planets have? Try and explain any pattern that you find.
(f) Which planets will go round the Sun more than once in your lifetime?

2 (a) Here is something active to do. You can make a model of the solar system. The scale of your solar system should be 1 m for 10 million kilometres. Use Table 1 to calculate how far each planet needs to be placed from the Sun. Now go outside and make your model – you will need a lot of space!
(b) Now work out where the nearest star, Alpha Centauri, should be placed on your model. Should it be in the next street, the next town or where? (Alpha Centauri is 6000 times further away from the Sun than Pluto is.)

3 Try and answer these questions about the solar system. You may need to go to a library to find the answers.
(a) Where is the Sea of Tranquillity?
(b) Which planet has a red spot?
(c) What are Oberon and Titania?
(d) What are 'asteroids'?
(e) Which planet has the shortest day?
(f) How many planets have rings around them?

THE FOUR SEASONS

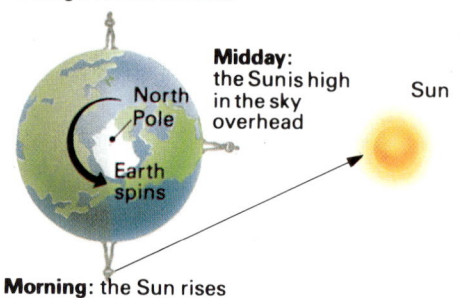

Evening: the Sun is setting over the horizon

Midday: the Sun is high in the sky overhead

Morning: the Sun rises and is seen low down close to the ground

Figure 1

The Earth spins around on its axis. It rotates once in about 24 hours. This is why we have days and nights. When we face the Sun it is day; and when we cannot see the Sun it is night. At night we can see stars. The stars are there all the time, but the sky is too bright for us to see them during the day.

Because the Earth spins, the Sun, Moon and stars seem to move across the sky. Figure 1 shows the Earth as you would see it from above the North Pole. Professor Chandrasekhar lives on the Equator. You can see from Figure 1 that the Professor sees the Sun close to the ground in the morning and evening, but that it is overhead at midday.

The Earth moves around the Sun in an approximately circular orbit. The closest the Earth gets to the Sun is 147 million kilometres; the furthest is 152 million kilometres. The Earth takes 365¼ days to complete its path round the Sun. This is why we have 365 days in our calendar. Every four years, we have a **leap year** with an extra day to make up for the ¼ day lost every year.

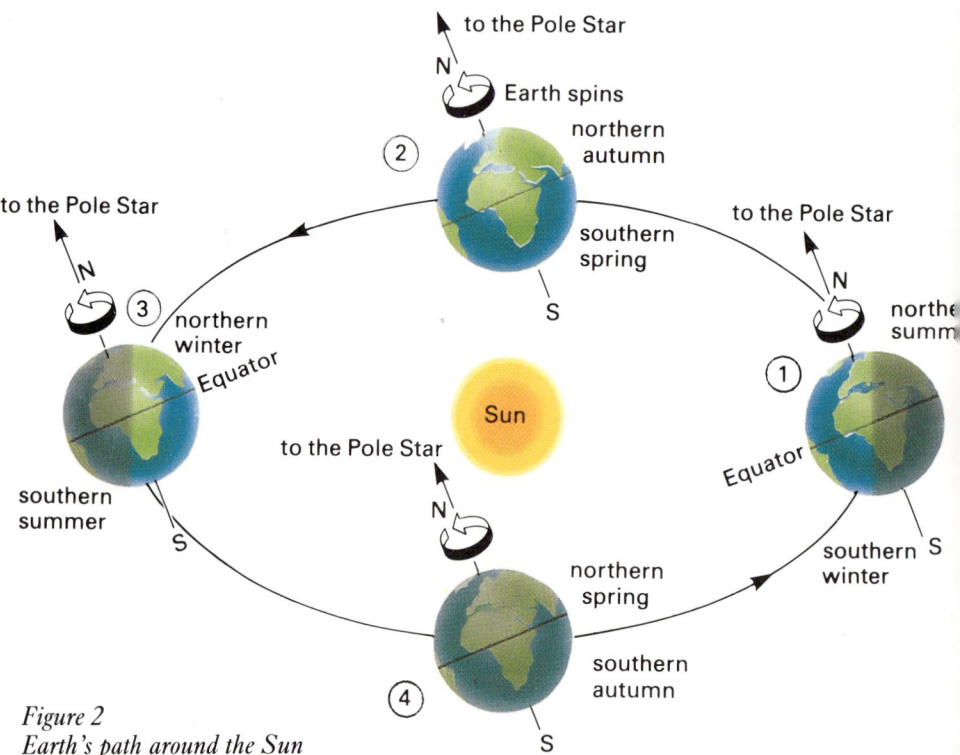

Figure 2
Earth's path around the Sun

Animals like the hedgehog in the photo hibernate over the winter. This reduces their energy demands to a low level so they can survive the cold months when food is scarce

Figure 2 shows the Earth's yearly path. The Earth spins around an axis that goes through the North and South Poles. All the time, the North Pole points towards the pole star (Polaris). The Earth's axis is tilted as shown in Figure 3. This tilt gives the Earth its seasons. In the middle of our summer the northern half of the Earth is tipped towards the Sun by an angle of 23½° (position (1) in Figure 2). At this time, the south of the Earth is tipped away from the Sun. Because the north is tipped towards the Sun it is hotter so it is summer. But the south is tipped away so it is cold and winter. Six months later, the Earth has reached position (3). The north is now tipped away from the Sun, and the south is tipped towards the Sun. It is now winter for us, and summer in the south. In the spring and autumn, the northern and southern halves of the Earth get equal amounts of sunshine.

The tilt of the Earth's axis also causes the length of our days to change. In Figure 3, you can see that it is summer in the north. Look at the half of the Earth north of the equator; more of it is in sunlight than in darkness. This makes our summer days long. More of the south is in darkness, so it has long winter nights. In the northern summer, the North Pole always sees the Sun, so it has 24 hours of daylight each day. But in the winter, the North Pole has no daylight at all. The Equator has days that are 12 hours long all through the year. If you live in Kenya, the Sun rises at 6 am every morning and sets at 6 pm; there is very little twilight. If you live in Oslo, you will get 20 hours of sunlight in the summer, but only four hours of sunlight in winter.

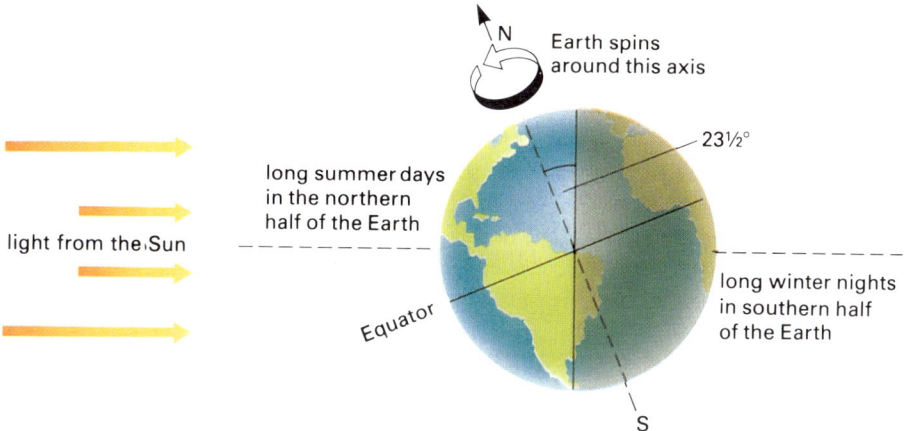

Figure 3

Figure 4
In winter, the Sun is low in the sky and shadows are long. In summer, the Sun is high in the sky and so shadows are shorter

QUESTIONS

1 Jo knows it is cold at the North Pole. But she thinks that, over a year, someone living at the North Pole would see the Sun for as long as someone living at the Equator. Is she right?

2 Imagine what it would be like on the Earth if it was tilted at a different angle. In the diagram on the left below, the Earth does not tilt at all. What happens then? Do we have different seasons? Do our days change in length? In the diagram on the right below, the North Pole is facing the Sun. Can you imagine what life would be like now?

3 Mars is quite similar to the Earth; its axis of rotation is tilted towards the sun by an angle of 24°, and its day is 24½ hours long.

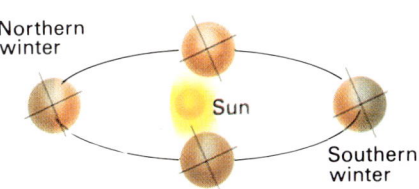

The diagram above shows Mars' orbit round the Sun. In southern winter it is 250 million km away from the Sun, but only 200 million km from the Sun in northern winter. Describe how the seasons on Mars differ from ours. Is a northern winter on Mars colder than a southern winter?

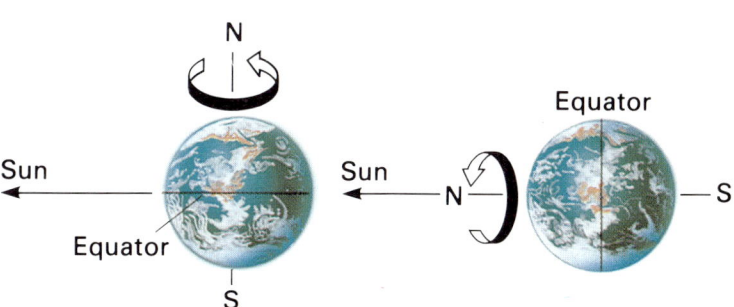

12 BEYOND THE SOLAR SYSTEM

Look at the sky on a dark night. How many stars do you think you can see? All of these stars are great distances away from us. We measure distances to stars in **light years**. A light year is the distance that light travels in one year. This is about 10 million million kilometres. The brightest star in the sky (after the Sun) is Sirius. It is also one of the nearest, but light takes nine years to reach us from Sirius. Light takes only six hours to reach Pluto from the Sun. This makes our solar system look very small.

Try to look at the sky on a clear night through binoculars or a small telescope. You will be able to see even more stars. You may be able to see the milky way. Many of the stars in the milky way have their own solar systems.

Clusters of millions of stars like the milky way are called galaxies. The Sun is one of the stars in the milky way (Figure 1). The milky way has about 100 000 million stars in it. If you could see our galaxy from the side, it would look like two fried eggs stuck back to back (Figure 1); it is long and thin except for a bulge in the middle. If you could see the galaxy from the top it would look like a giant whirlpool with great spiral arms. In fact, the galaxy does spin round. Our Sun takes about 220 million years to go once round the centre of the galaxy. In your life time, the pattern of stars that you see each night will not appear to change. But over thousands of years the pattern will change as our Sun moves through the galaxy. Our ancestors who lived 100 000 years ago would have seen different constellations from those we can see today.

From the Earth, we see the stars of our galaxy as the milky way

This spiral galaxy is in the constellation of Pisces. It is at a distance of 30 million light years and has a diameter of 80 thousand light years

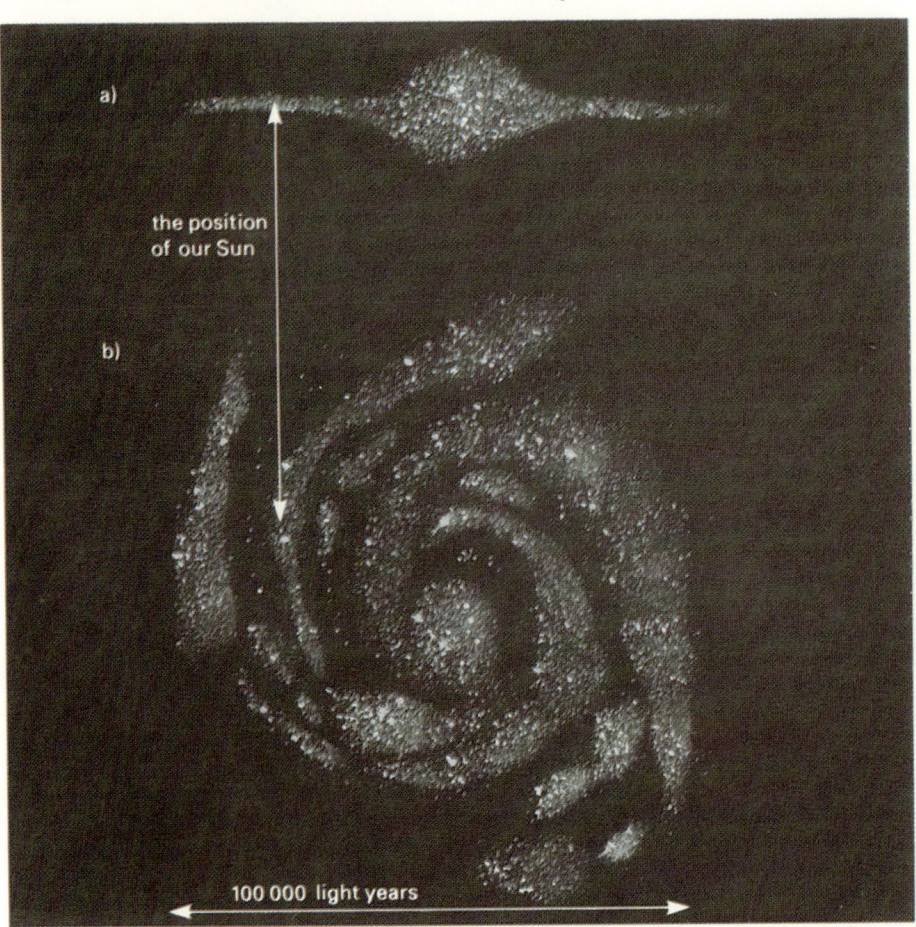

Figure 1
(a) Side view of our galaxy
(b) Top view of our galaxy
(If you look towards the centre of our galaxy, you see the milky way. On dark summer nights, this looks like a milky band overhead, but it is made from billions of stars)

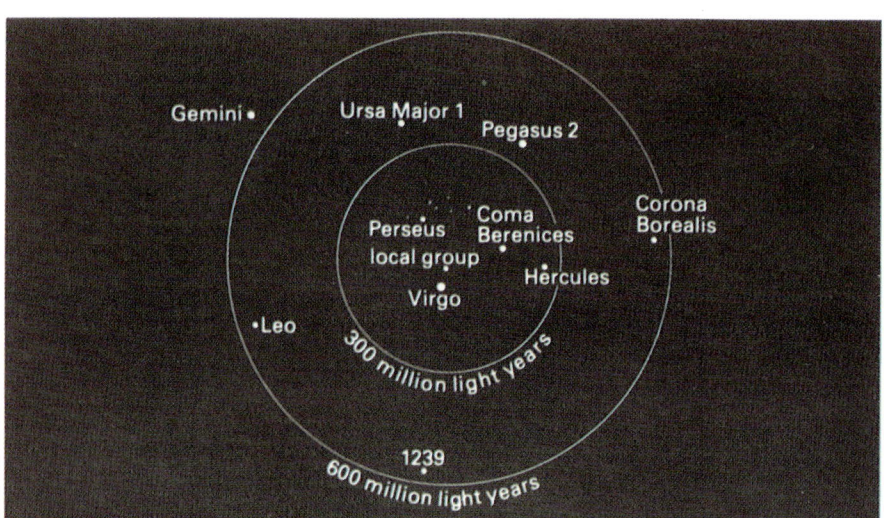

Figure 2
This map shows groups of galaxies close to our local group. The most distant galaxies in the universe are 15 000 million light years away from us. In this map, a large dot means that the group of galaxies contains more than 50 galaxies

About 10 000 million years ago there were no galaxies at all, and the universe was full of hydrogen and helium gas. **Gravity** is a force which acts over enormous distances, even over thousands of millions of light years. Groups of galaxies were formed when gravity gradually pulled large volumes of gas together. After the galaxies were formed, stars were formed inside the galaxies. Look at Figure 2. This shows a map of groups of galaxies. Our local group is in the middle. There are about 20 galaxies in our local group. Some groups of galaxies have as many as 1000 galaxies in them. There is a total of about 10 000 million galaxies in the universe.

This photograph shows part of the Virgo cluster of galaxies. The Virgo cluster is about 50 million light years away. It contains about 1000 galaxies

QUESTIONS

1 Explain what is meant by each of the following terms.
(a) moon, (b) planet, (c) star, (d) galaxy, (e) group of galaxies, (f) universe

2 Our Sun is about 4600 million years old. Use the information in the text to calculate the number of times the Sun has rotated round the galaxy. Humans have existed on the earth for about 50 000 years; how many times round the galaxy has the Sun rotated in that time?

3 One of the nearest galaxies to us is the Andromeda galaxy. It is 2 million light years away. The fastest rocket we can make travels at $1/10\,000$ of the speed of light. Calculate how long it would take us to reach Andromeda. (The speed of light is 300 000 km/s.)

13 MOVING PLANETS

Figure 1
The Earth moves in an elliptical orbit round the Sun. The Moon moves around the Earth

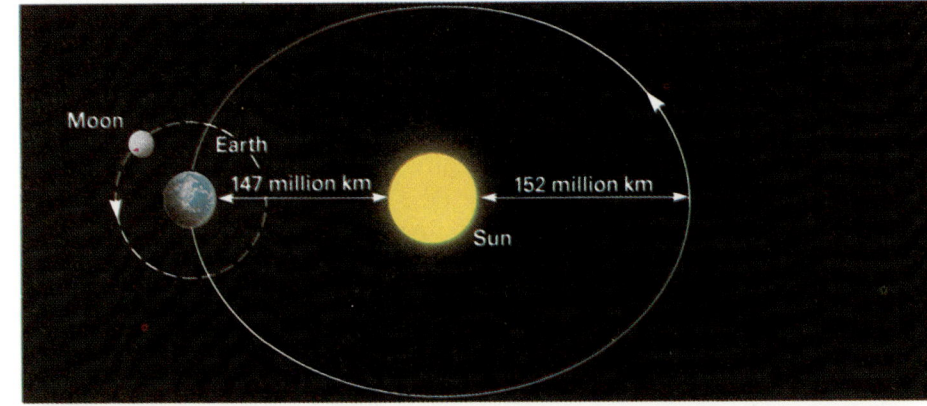

The Earth moves round the Sun in a curved path. The shape of this path is an **ellipse**. The ellipse is a bit like a squashed circle. Figure 1 shows how the Earth and Moon move together round the Sun. All the planets move in elliptical paths around the Sun. They all move in the same direction, as shown in Figure 2. The planets near the Sun move faster than those further away. In Figure 2 you are looking down on the solar system from on top. If you could look at it from the side (Figure 3), you would see all the planets in nearly the same plane. This is called the **plane of the ecliptic**. Our Moon also lies in the same plane. This means that you can quite often see the Moon close to some planets in the sky.

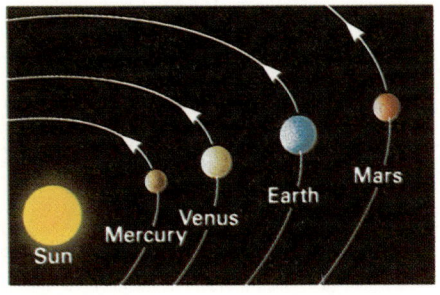

Figure 2
All planets rotate around the Sun in the same direction

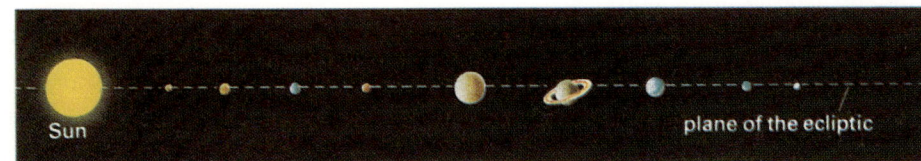

Figure 3
All planets lie very close to the same plane. Will all planets always be on the same side of the Sun?

In ancient Rome, the word 'planet' meant 'wanderer'. The planets were given their name because they appear to wander around the sky. The Earth moves round the Sun once a year. In July, we are always in the same position so we see the same stars at night each year. The stars are so far away that they do not appear to move at all, even over thousands of years. Each July we see the bright star Antares low in the sky. From 1984 to 1988, Saturn could be seen clearly on July evenings close to Antares. But Saturn moves slowly round the Sun, taking about 30 years to go once round (Figure 4). During 1986 and 1987 Saturn moved slowly past Antares (Figure 5).

Yearly motion

Figure 5 shows Saturn's passage through the stars over a period of several years. However, by looking at Saturn's position at the same time each year, the effect of the Earth's motion has been ignored. When you look at a planet every month or so, you will see a more complicated motion.

Figure 4
As Saturn moves slowly round the Sun, we see it move against the stars

EARTH AND SPACE

Figure 6 shows how Mars moved past the Hyades and Pleiades in late 1990 and early 1991. Notice that Mars moved to the left for most of the time; but between October and December it moved backwards, through a **retrograde loop**. This loop occurs because the Earth, which orbits the Sun faster than Mars, overtakes Mars at this point.

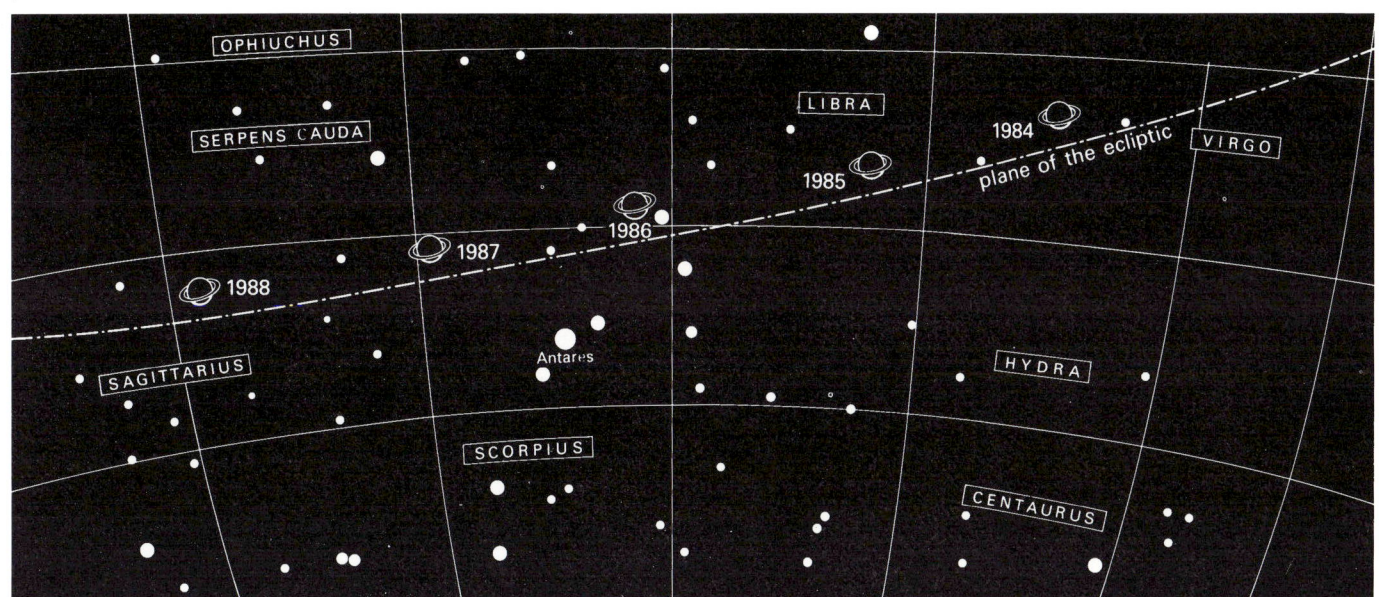

Figure 5
This is how Saturn moved over a period of 5 years

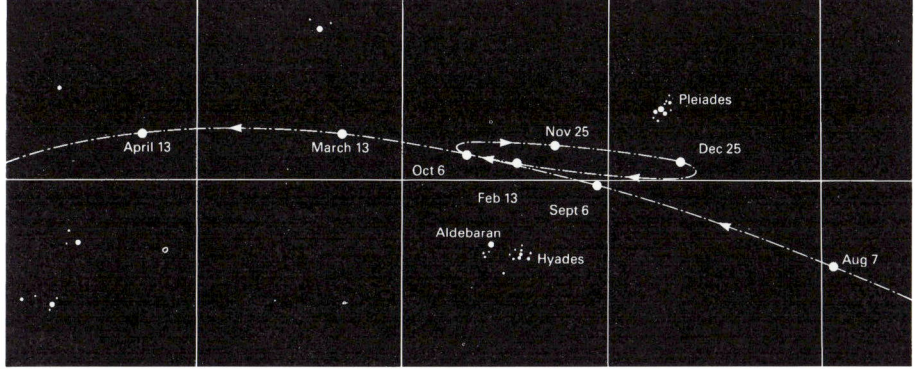

Figure 6
The movement of Mars during 1990 and 1991

QUESTIONS

1 (a) Look at the star map in Figure 5. Approximately where will you see Saturn in 2014? (Remember Saturn takes about 30 years to go round the Sun.)
(b) Explain why it will be very difficult to see Saturn in July 2001. In which month will it be best to see Saturn in 2001?

2 If you look at Jupiter or Saturn through a telescope, you can see a large planet with clear markings. If you look at Pluto through a telescope it looks like a star – a small point of light. Pluto was discovered in 1930. How did astronomers know that Pluto is a planet and not a fixed star?

3 (a) Make a copy of Figure 4. Draw lines from Earth positions 1, 2 and 3 to Saturn's position in 1986. Use your diagram to explain why Saturn appears to go through a backward loop every year.
(b) Explain why Mars appears to move more rapidly than Saturn.

4 Prepare a five-minute talk for the class on 'planetary motion'.

14 GRAVITATION

Newton's law of gravity

In the 100 years before Isaac Newton was born, astronomers had carefully observed the motion of planets and the positions of stars. From these measurements, the astronomers worked out that the Sun is the centre of our solar system, and that the planets move in orbits around it. But nobody understood what kept the planets moving along their paths.

In 1665, the great plague swept across England. Cambridge University was closed and all the students, including Newton, were sent home. It was then, stranded in Lincolnshire, that Newton worked out his Law of Gravity. He suddenly realised that the Earth's gravitational pull does more than keep our feet on the ground. It reaches out, beyond the highest mountains, and into the depths of space. The Earth's pull stretches 400 000 km across space, and keeps the Moon moving around us.

Newton said that any two masses in the universe attract each other with a gravitational pull. The size of this force is given by:

$$F = \frac{GM_1 M_2}{R^2}$$

Sir Isaac Newton (1642–1727) was the first person to realise that the Earth's gravitational pull extended beyond the highest mountains. He used his theory to explain the Moon's motion

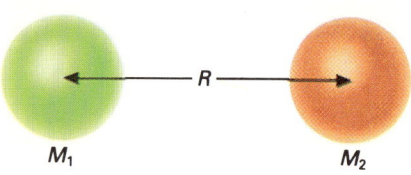

Figure 1

F is the force (in newtons) between two masses, M_1 and M_2 (in kg). These masses might be planets for example. R is the distance between the centre of these masses (in m), see Figure 1. G ('big gee') is the universal constant of gravitation; its value is 6.7×10^{-11} Nm^2/kg^2. The pull is too weak to be noticeable between two people. It is only when one of the masses is the size of a planet that we can feel the force of gravity.

Newton's equation shows us that the Earth's pull gets weaker the further out into space we go (Figure 2). What is the Earth's pull on the Moon? The Moon is 60 times further from the centre of the Earth than we are. For us, the pull is 10 N/kg – each kg experiences a pull of 10 N. In the equation, if R gets 60 times bigger, $1/R^2$ get 60^2, or 3600, times smaller. So the Earth exerts a pull of $^{10}/_{3600}$ N on each kg of the moon; that is about 0.003 N/kg.

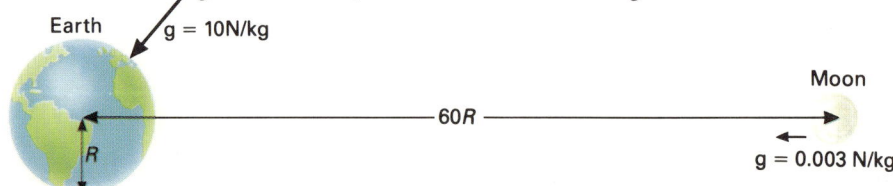

Figure 2
The Earth's pull gets weaker further away, but it is strong enough to keep the Moon in orbit around us

Orbits

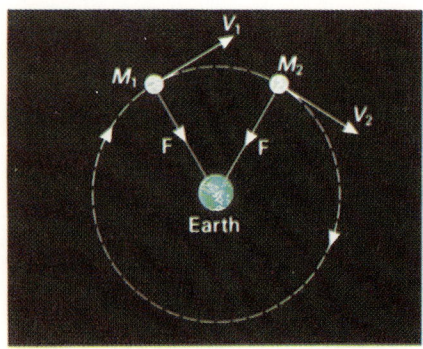

Figure 3
The Earth's pull changes the velocity of the Moon from v_1 to v_2

Figure 3 shows the Moon's orbit round the Earth; in position M_1, the moon is moving along the direction v_1. Without any force acting on it, the Moon would continue to move in that direction. But the Earth is always pulling the Moon towards it. This pull is at right-angles to the Moon's motion. The pull does not speed the Moon up; the pull deflects the Moon away from a straight path, into a curved path. At M_2, the Moon has a new velocity v_2. The Earth's pull changes this velocity again. The Earth pulls on the Moon all the way round its orbit.

The Moon has stayed in orbit for billions of years. As it goes round the Earth it does not lose any energy. There are no frictional forces in space to slow it down. The Earth's force on the Moon does not change its speed, because it acts at right-angles to its motion.

Tides

The gravitational pull of the Moon on the ocean causes our **tides**. We get two high tides a day. The Earth-Moon system rotates about a centre of gravity (or **barycentre**) at B (Figure 4). This is inside the Earth but not at its centre. At A, there is a high tide because the Moon pulls more strongly on the water closer to it. At C there is also a high tide. At C the Moon pulls the water less strongly. As the water rotates around B it piles up; this is because the Moon's pull is not strong enough to keep it in a smaller circular path.

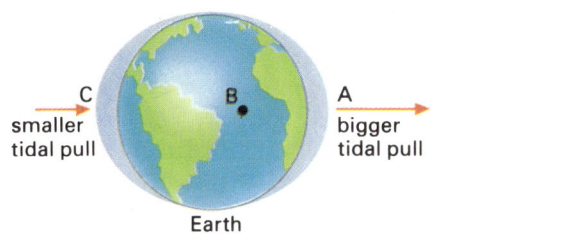

Figure 4
The tidal pulls are exaggerated here; the height of the tides is only a few metres

The Sun also exerts a tidal pull on our seas, but about ½ as much as the Moon. Twice a month, the Sun and Moon line up to produce a large tidal pull. We then get **spring tides**. When the Sun and Moon pull at right-angles to each other, the high tides are smaller. These are called **neap tides** (Figure 5). Other factors, such as strong winds, also affect the height of tides.

This photograph by the Voyager 1 spacecraft shows Io (left) and Europa above the swirling clouds of Jupiter. Newton also used his theory to explain that all planets (and stars) have their own gravitational pulls. Jupiter pulls its moons to keep them in orbit. The Sun pulls the planets to keep them in orbit too

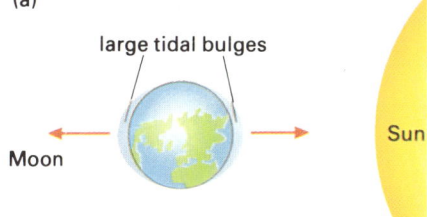

Spring tides occur at full moons (above) and new moons (below)

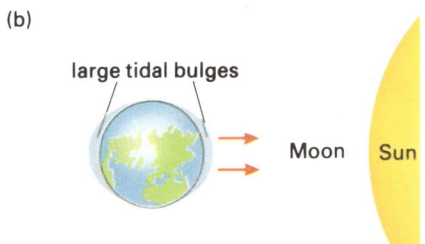

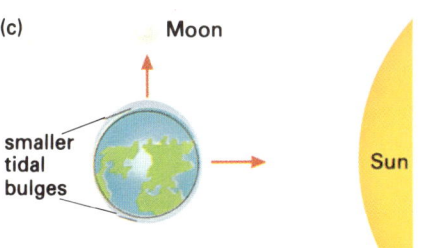

Figure 5
Neap tides occur when the Sun and Moon pull at right angles to each other

QUESTIONS

1 Jupiter is 325 times as massive as the Earth, and Jupiter is five times further away from the Sun than we are. Calculate the ratio of the Sun's pull on Jupiter to the Sun's pull on the Earth.

2 Explain carefully how Newton's law can account for the orbital motion of satellites around the Earth.

3 On 21 March, the morning high tide at Plymouth was at 0818 hours. On 22 March, the morning high tide was at 0900 hours. Can you explain why? (Hint: the Moon takes about 29 days to go around us.)

4 Use Newton's equation to calculate the gravitational forces on Sarah, who has a mass of 50 kg, in these places: (a) on Earth, (b) on Mars, (c) on the Moon. You will need the data below.

- Mass of Earth 6×10^{24} kg
- Mass of Moon 7×10^{22} kg
- Mass of Mars 6×10^{23} kg
- Radius of Earth 6.4×10^{6} m
- Radius of Mars 3.4×10^{6} m
- Radius of Moon 1.7×10^{6} m
- $G = 6.7 \times 10^{-11}$ Nm²/kg²

15 MAKING A STAR

A 'nebula' means a fuzzy or blurred object – nebulas look blurred through a telescope. In the Orion nebula, hydrogen gas condenses to form stars. In the middle you can see a group of four stars; they are called the 'trapezium'. The middle of the nebula is lit up by bright young stars, which are only about 300 000 years old

Like all stars, our Sun was formed from a giant cloud of gas. The photograph opposite shows part of the **orion nebula**, where stars are being formed now. The orion nebula is made mostly from hydrogen gas. The density of the gas is very low – about 100 million million times less dense than water. However, over millions of years, gravity acts to condense the gas into a smaller volume. This warms the gas up. As the gas atoms fall towards each other they speed up; potential energy is turned into kinetic energy. When the atoms collide, their large kinetic energy is turned into heat energy. Eventually, the temperature at the centre of the ball of gas reaches 15 million K and a star is born (Figure 1).

Nuclear fusion

Once the inside of a star reaches a temperature of about 15 million K, nuclear fusion starts. Like the cloud of gas that made it, a star is made mostly of hydrogen. At very high temperatures the hydrogen atoms are ripped apart, leaving only protons and electrons inside the star. At low temperatures two protons cannot collide because their charges repel each other. But at the very high temperatures inside stars, two protons have enough energy to overcome this repulsion. When two protons collide they can join or fuse together. By this process of fusion, protons join to form helium nuclei (Figure 2). The fusion of nuclei releases a lot of energy. This is how stars produce their heat and light.

Our Sun is half way through its life of 10 thousand million years. Throughout its life, the Sun has burnt fairly constantly. This is why life has evolved on our planet, the temperature has been steady. However it seems possible that, from time to time, the Sun's output of energy might change by a very small amount. In the second half of the seventeenth century, the climate was very harsh. The Thames froze over during winter. It is possible that the Ice Ages were caused by a decline in solar power output.

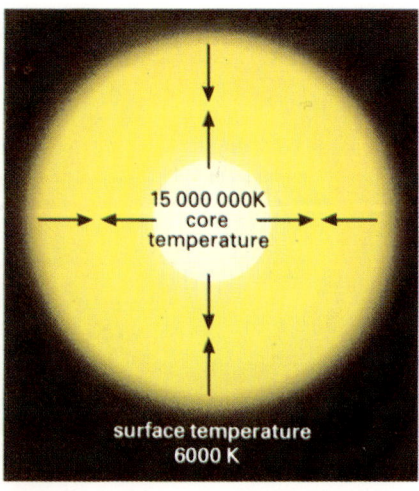

Figure 1
A star is a battle ground. The forces of gravity try to collapse a star, but these inward forces are balanced by the enormous outward pressure exerted by the hot core. The pressure at the centre of the star is about 500 million times bigger than the Earth's atmospheric pressure

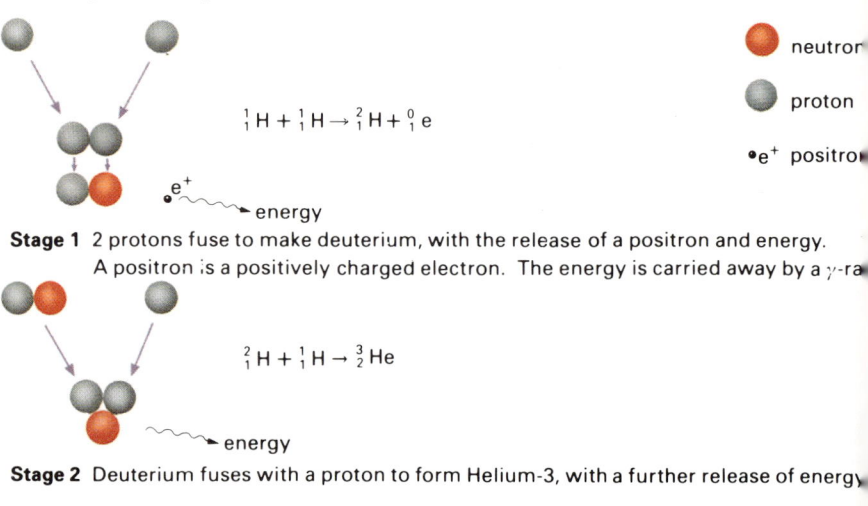

Stage 1 2 protons fuse to make deuterium, with the release of a positron and energy. A positron is a positively charged electron. The energy is carried away by a γ-ray

$${}^2_1H + {}^1_1H \rightarrow {}^3_2He$$

Stage 2 Deuterium fuses with a proton to form Helium-3, with a further release of energy

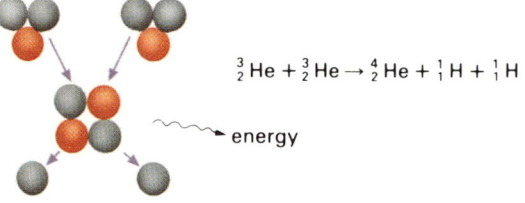

Stage 3 The process is completed when 2 Helium-3 nuclei fuse to make Helium-4.

Figure 2
Nuclear fusion in the Sun

A dying Sun

Eventually the hydrogen in the Sun will run out. Without the high pressure in its centre sustained by nuclear fusion the Sun will collapse. This rapid collapse will warm the core further at 100 million K.

At this temperature the helium nuclei can fuse to make heavier elements. The Sun will swell up and turn into a red giant, with a diameter 100 times bigger than it is now. The Sun will swallow up Mercury, and the Earth will be burnt to a cinder. Later the Sun will collapse again and finish its life as a tiny white dwarf star, before cooling down like a dying fire.

Some stars 'die' in a more dramatic way. Stars that are about four times as massive as our Sun collapse so rapidly at the end of their lives that they turn into **black holes**. The gravitational pull of a black hole is so strong that not even light can escape from it (Figure 3). Stars that are about 10 times as massive as the Sun (blue giants) live brilliant but short lives; they live for about 10 million years only. In that time, they shine more brightly than 10 000 suns. When they die they blow themselves apart in a **supernova explosion**. A supernova is so bright that it can outshine a whole galaxy of stars. Heavy elements are made in supernovas; our own solar system would have been made from the remnants of such an explosion. You are made from a recycled star.

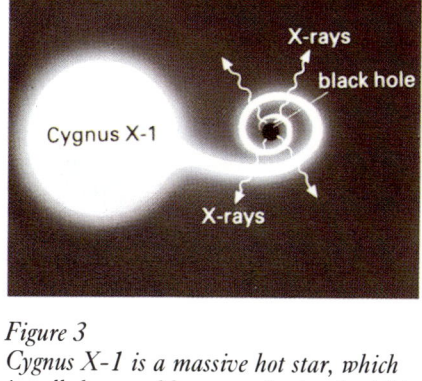

Figure 3
Cygnus X-1 is a massive hot star, which is pulled around by a massive but invisible dark companion. The companion is as heavy as four suns. The companion is thought to be a black hole, which sucks matter out of its neighbouring star. As matter falls into the black hole, X-rays are emitted

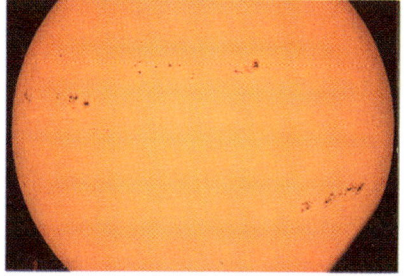

We think there are more sun spots when the Sun is hot. At the end of the seventeenth century, no sunspots were seen for about 60 years. This coincided with a 'mini' Ice Age

The bright star Sandulek-69 turned into a supernova in January 1987. 'Supernova' means bright and new. A supernova is a dying star, but it shines brightly where people had not previously seen a star. The star outshone the whole of the Magellan Cloud which is Sandulek's galaxy

QUESTIONS

1 Explain carefully how stars are formed. Why do stars heat up when they are formed?

2 (a) Explain what is meant by 'nuclear fusion'.
(b) Why can nuclear fusion only occur at high temperatures?
(c) What is deuterium?

3 (a) How do black holes form?
(b) What is a 'supernova'? How does it get its name?

4 Blue giants live for 10 million years. This is described in the text as a 'short time'; why?

5 Look at the table of data about some stars. Then answer the questions that follow.

Star	Temperature at surface (°C)	Diameter relative to Sun	Mass relative to Sun	Brightness relative to Sun
Antares	3100	300	15	2500
Rigel	30 000	10	30	25 000
β-Centauri	19 000	6	4	4000
Vega	10 600	2.6	3	40
Sun	5800	1	1	1
61 Cygni	3900	0.7	0.5	0.1
Sirius B	9000	0.03	1	0.002

(a) Is there a connection between the brightness of a star and its temperature?
(b) Is there a connection between the brightness of a star and its diameter?
(c) Can you work out which star is a red giant?
(d) Can you work out which star is a white dwarf?
(e) Can you work out which star is a blue giant?

16 THE HERTZSPRUNG-RUSSELL DIAGRAM

The Hertzsprung-Russell diagram

When you look at the sky at night, you can see stars with many different colours. These stars also have a wide range of brightness. The first astronomers to realise that the brightness of a star was related to its colour were Ejnar Hertzsprung and Henry Russell. They introduced the idea of plotting a graph of the brightness or luminosity of a star against the star's colour. Figure 1 shows such a graph, which is called a Hertzsprung–Russell diagram. Each point represents a star.

Most stars are grouped along a band stretching from the top left to the lower right of the diagram. This band is called the main sequence. The Sun occurs roughly in the middle of the main sequence. The most striking feature of the diagram is that the brightest and hottest stars are blue or white, and the dullest and coldest stars are red. Russell and Hertzsprung also discovered that there are very bright orange and red stars; these are giants and supergiants, which form a separate branch at an angle to the main sequence. Besides these stars there are also some white dwarf stars. The Hertzsprung–Russell diagram shown here gives a slightly distorted picture of the relative numbers of different types of star. You might have got the impression that the sky is full of giant stars. In fact, the Sun is larger than most stars. Only 5% of stars are bigger than the Sun and only 0.05% of stars are giants. However, giants are easy to see at great distances, because they outshine by far all other stars. The relatively small number of stars larger than our Sun, provide over 95% of a galaxy's light output. You can see this clearly in the photograph of the galaxy NGC 253. This galaxy lies about 10 million light years away from us, yet you can clearly pick out blue and red supergiants which shine out like beacons.

Spiral Galaxy NGC 253. In this photograph you can pick out red and blue giants which outshine other stars in the galaxy

Figure 1 The Hertzsprung–Russell diagram

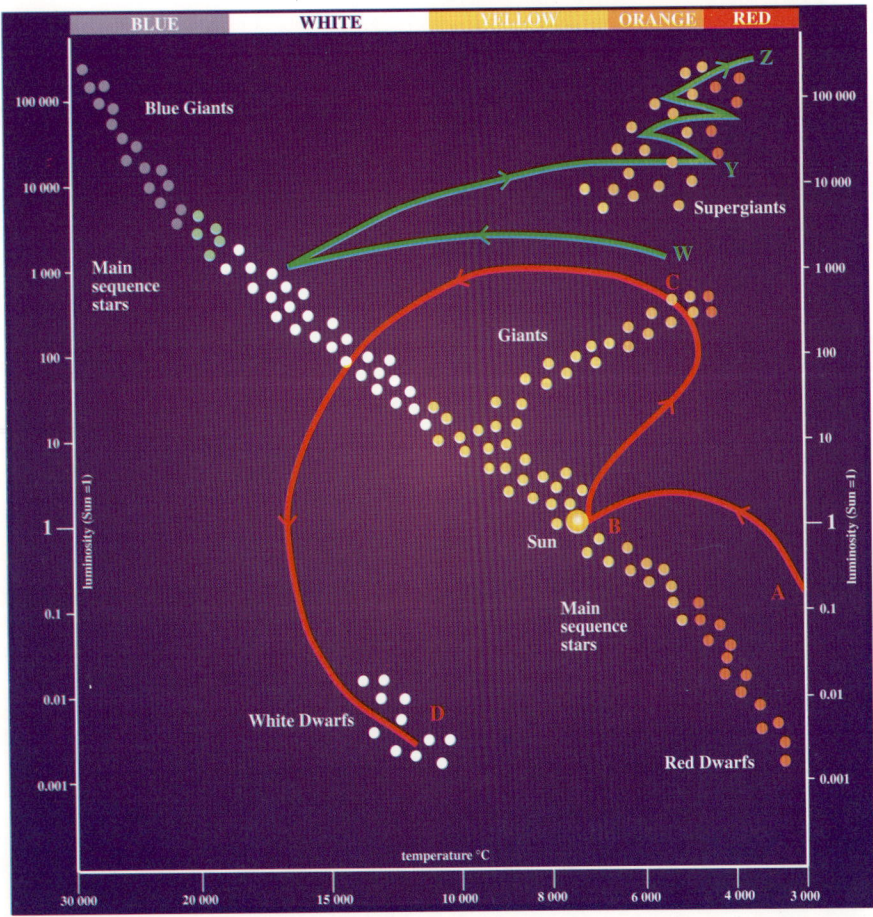

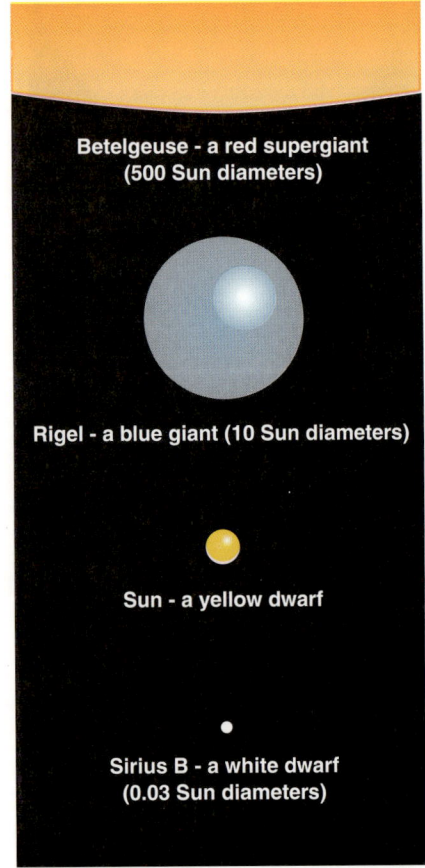

Figure 2 Stars come in all sizes

Star lifetimes

The red line on the Hertzsprung–Russell diagram shows the evolutionary path of the Sun. At A it is collapsing out of a huge cloud of gas. B is its present position on the main sequence. The Sun has already been a main sequence star for about 4.6 thousand million years; it is about half way through its life. During its lifetime, a main sequence star converts hydrogen to helium by the process of thermonuclear fusion (see page 36). The main sequence lifetime of a star depends on two factors: the mass and luminosity (or brightness) of the star. If a star is very bright it uses its hydrogen up very quickly, and a more massive star has more hydrogen for the fusion process. To take an example, look at the table. A blue giant 15 times as massive as the Sun is 15 000 times as bright. This means it is using hydrogen 15 000 times as rapidly as the Sun, but it has 15 times as much to provide. Its lifetime, therefore is 15/15 000 × the Sun's lifetime, which is only 10 million years. At the other extreme, a red dwarf glows very dimly, but lives for 2000 times longer than the Sun.

Eventually, the Sun's hydrogen will run out. Without the high pressure in its core maintained by nuclear fusion it will collapse. This collapse warms the Sun's core further to a temperature of 100 million K. At this temperature helium nuclei fuse to make heavier elements such as oxygen and carbon. The Sun will swell up into a red giant with a diameter 100 times bigger than now. Its increase in size will be accompanied by a huge increase in brightness. The Sun will live only briefly as a red giant – some 10 million years or so. Because the lifetime of a giant is much less than that of a main sequence star, there are fewer of them to be seen. The Sun will end its life as a white dwarf, before cooling down like a dying fire.

The green line shows the evolutionary path of a star 1000 times brighter than the Sun. It settles onto the main sequence for about 100 million years. When its hydrogen runs out it expands, but now into a supergiant. These supergiants pass through a series of expansions and contractions growing brighter at every stage. Finally, these stars blow themselves apart. Some are seen as novas – bright new stars. Others become supernovas where a star is completely destroyed. A supernova is so bright that it outshines an entire galaxy of 100 thousand million stars.

This group of stars is known as the Jewel Box. Most of the stars in the group are blue giants, but one star has progressed to the red giant stage

QUESTIONS

1 (a) Explain what is meant by a Hertzsprung–Russell diagram. Describe its main features.
(b) What is a main sequence star?

2 Only 5% of all stars are brighter than the Sun. Use the table of lifetimes and luminosities to explain why there are fewer bright stars than there are dull stars.

3 (a) The lifetime, T, of a main sequence star (in thousand millions of years) can be calculated using the formula:

$$T = \frac{10M}{L}$$

M is the star's mass relative to the Sun, and L is the star's luminosity relative to the Sun: ie. for the Sun $M = 1$, $L = 1$.

Explain why the lifetime is proportional to the star's mass, and inversely proportional to the star's luminosity.
(b) Use the formula to fill in the gaps in the table.
(c) The brightest known star is S-Doradus in the Magellan Clouds. It is thought to be about 1 million times brighter than our Sun and 50 times as massive. Explain why there are so few stars as bright as this.

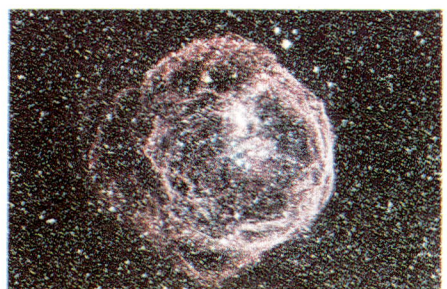

This is the remnants of an ancient supernova. Over thousands of years the star has been scattered wide across space

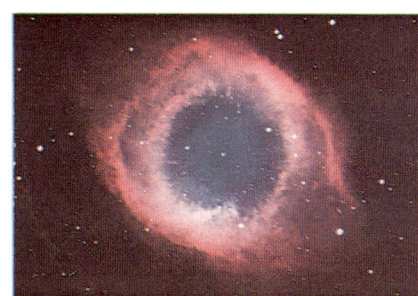

This star ended its life as a nova, briefly flaring up and losing some of its outer layers

Mass of star (Sun = 1)	15	10	5	3	2	1	0.5	0.2
Lifetime of star (thousand millions of years)	0.01	0.02		0.23	0.7	10		20 000
Luminosity of star (Sun = 1)	15 000	5 000	700	130		1	0.1	0.001

Table 1   The life time of main sequence stars

17 THE PLANETS

This photograph shows Saturn with two moons and its rings. Notice the shadows cast by the rings and one of the moons. The gap between A and B rings is known as the Cassini Division

The planets: their development and composition

Most scientific theories are developed as a result of experiment or observations. There are a few theories about the development of the solar system. However, they are quite speculative because we cannot observe other solar systems forming. Astronomers think that about one third of all stars have planets, but our telescopes cannot show them. Figure 1 shows a popular theory for the development of the solar system. The planets, Sun and moons are thought to have developed at the same time (about 4500 million years ago) out of a large gaseous cloud.

The Sun is made mostly from hydrogen and helium, but there are traces of other elements too. The composition of the planets can be split into three classes, depending on their volatility: **rocky**, **icy** and **gaseous**. Rocks are mostly iron, and oxides and silicates of magnesium, calcium and aluminium. There are however many other elements present in all planets too, but in lesser abundance. The gases present in planets are mostly hydrogen and helium, then oxygen, nitrogen, ammonia, carbon dioxide and methane. Water ice is the commonest icy material, but there are also solid and liquid gases to be found. For example, the polar caps on Mars are thought to contain a lot of solid carbon dioxide; the atmosphere of Jupiter contains water and ammonia ice.

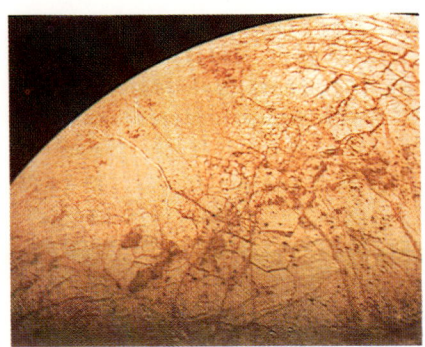

On Europa, one of the moons of Jupiter, ice floes have covered the volcanic craters on the surface

1 4500 million years ago a shock wave, in a spiral arm of our galaxy, triggered the collapse of a gas cloud. This developed into a doughnut shape, which flattened out.

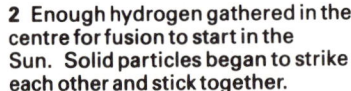

2 Enough hydrogen gathered in the centre for fusion to start in the Sun. Solid particles began to strike each other and stick together.

3 Eventually, as the small particles continued to coalesce, just a few large planets and moons were left. Most of the gas and dust in the solar system became attached to a planet, or was removed by a strong solar wind. After millions of years, the gravitational attraction between the planets tended to pull their orbits into the same plane.

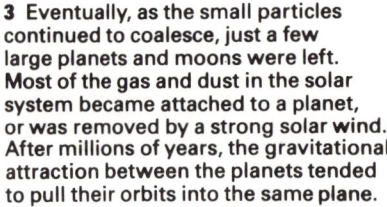

Figure 1

The composition of a planet depends very much on its position in the solar system. The planets close to the Sun have a very different composition to those further away. Table 1 summarises the composition of the planets, and Figure 2 their internal structures.

Planet	Mass relative to Earth	Radius (Earth = 1)	Relative density (water = 1)	Distance from Sun in A.U.[†]	% Rocks	% Ice	% Gas	Main gases in atmosphere
Mercury	0.06	0.38	5.4	0.39	nearly all	–	–	none
Venus	0.82	0.95	5.2	0.72	nearly all	–	some in atmosphere	CO_2
Earth	1	1	5.5	1	nearly all	water in oceans, ice at poles	some in atmosphere	N_2 O_2
Mars	0.11	0.53	3.9	1.5	nearly all	ice at poles	some in atmosphere	CO_2
Jupiter	318	11.2	1.3	5.2	10% rock/ice		90%	H_2 He
Saturn	95	9.4	0.7	9.5	30% rock/ice		70%	H_2 He
Uranus	14.6	4.1	1.2	19.1	70% rock/ice		30%	H_2, He CH_4
Neptune	17.2	3.9	1.7	30.1	70% rock/ice		30%	H_2, He CH_4
Pluto	0.1?	0.4?	?	39.4	mostly rock/ice		?	none?

[†]1 Astronomical Unit or A.U. is the average Earth–Sun distance.
O_2: oxygen, N_2: nitrogen, CH_4: methane, CO_2: carbon dioxide.

Table 1

Figure 2

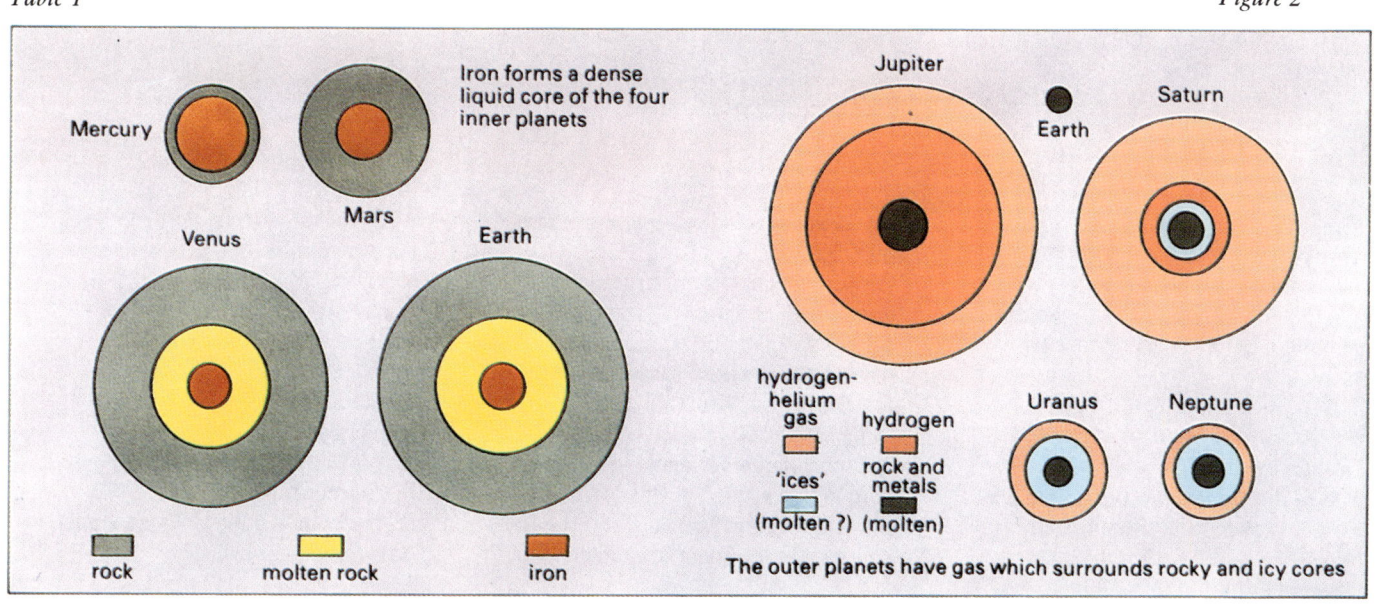

42 THE PLANETS

As Voyager flew past Io in March 1979, the cameras caught a volcano as it erupted. This photograph shows a huge plume of material thrown out into space

You should realise that there remains considerable doubt over the planets' exact structure and composition. The four inner planets are rocky. The four large giant planets have rocky and icy cores, but have large amounts of gas in their outer parts. Moons of Earth and Mars are rocky. The moons of the outer planets usually contain a considerable proportion of ice as well as rock. A possible explanation for the composition of the planets is as follows. In its early stages, the Sun was a lot hotter than it is now. The Sun lost a lot of material as a strong solar wind, which removed most of the gas from the inner planets.

Early in the life of the solar system, there were millions of small rocks still whizzing around. Some are still in orbit around the Sun, but most have collided with planets or moons. Mercury, Mars and many moons show the 'impact craters' caused by these rocks. Many of these craters are thought to be 4000 million years old, nearly as old as the solar system. The action of the Earth's atmosphere has eroded away craters. On the Moon and Mars, lava flows from volcanoes have covered over some craters, leaving flat plains. The volcanoes on Mars show that the planet was recently geologically active. Although there are no active volcanoes on the Moon, seismometers left there by the Apollo astronauts have detected small **moonquakes**. Io and Europa, two moons of Jupiter, are very active. Both are squeezed by Jupiter's strong gravitational field as they orbit, which generates a lot of heat. On Io, this heat results in many active volcanoes. On Europa, recent ice floes from beneath the surface have covered up the craters.

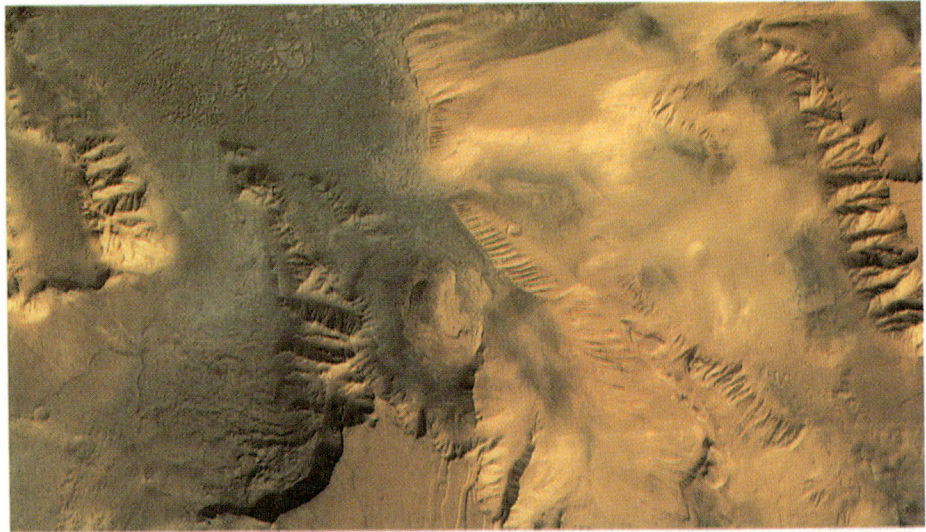

Mosaic of Viking orbiter photos showing the central portion of the giant Martian canyon system, the Valles Marineris. The layered terrain to the left of the image may have been formed by a huge, ancient lake

QUESTIONS

1 (a) In the second paragraph, the words *volatility* and *abundance* are used. What do these words mean?
(b) Explain why theories about the formation of the solar system are 'speculative'.

2 Mars has craters on its surface, but few craters are seen near volcanoes. Explain why.

3 Use the information in Table 1 and Figure 2 to answer these questions.
(a) Why are the four inner planets denser than the outer planets?
(b) What makes Neptune more dense than Saturn?
(c) Jupiter contains a larger proportion of gas than Saturn. Yet Jupiter is denser than Saturn. Account for this in terms of the planets' masses.
(d) Mars and Mercury are nearly the same size, yet Mercury is denser. Account for this in terms of their compositions.
(e) Which two planets are (i) the most similar, (ii) the most dissimilar?

4 Go to the library, do some research and write a short article on one of the following:
(a) the moons of Jupiter,
(b) the rings of Saturn,
(c) Uranus and Neptune,
(d) the atmosphere of Venus,
(e) Mars,
(f) rills and craters on the Moon,
(g) Mercury,
(h) the composition of Jupiter and Saturn.

18 SUN, STAND STILL!

Earth at the centre

Look at Figure 1. This shows how Pythagoras thought the Earth fitted into space in about 500 BC. He realised (correctly) that the Earth is a sphere. His model (incorrectly) places the Earth at the centre of the universe. The Earth was thought to be surrounded by several **crystal spheres** which carried the heavenly bodies. The outer **celestial** sphere carried the stars. To explain the motion of the stars, Pythagoras said that this sphere rotated once every 24 hours around a stationary Earth. The inner spheres rotated at slightly slower speeds. This allowed Pythagoras to explain the motion of the Moon, Sun and planets reasonably well.

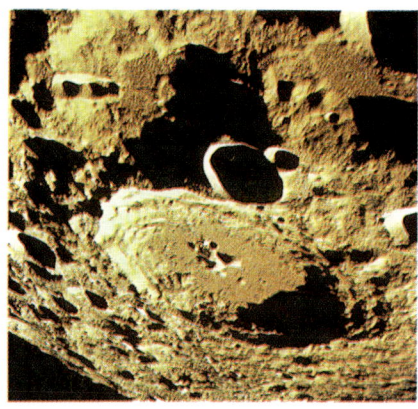

The Moon was formed 4600 million years ago at which time its surface was made of molten rock. There was a large number of meteors whizzing around in space then. The Moon was bombarded by some of these meteors, which caused the cratered surface we see today

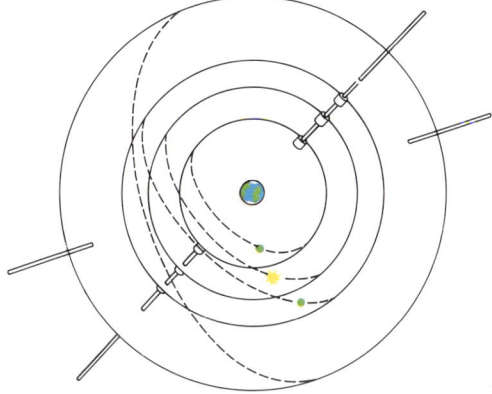

Figure 1
In 500 BC, the Greek philosophers thought heavenly bodies rotated round the Earth on crystal spheres. The stars are on the outer sphere

However, Pythagoras could not explain why some planets appear to make strange loops. Look at Figure 2. This shows how Jupiter appeared to move past the stars in 1991–2.

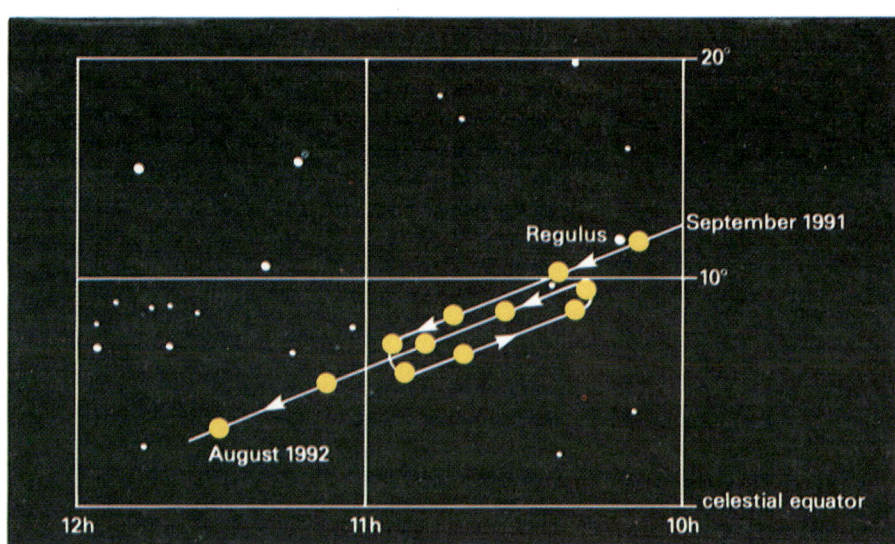

Figure 2
This diagram shows Jupiter's retrograde loop during 1991 and 1992. Jupiter is marked at intervals of one month

Jupiter's red spot has been a feature of its atmosphere for well over a hundred years. The spot is surrounded by swirling clouds blown around by winds of hurricane strength, with speeds in excess of 300 km per hour

Ptolemy (AD 120) produced another model to account for this motion (Figure 3). The arm EA rotates around the Earth every 12 years (in Jupiter's case). The arm AJ rotates around A once a year. The combined motion gives a looping movement. This model was only a calculating machine. It predicted very accurately the positions of planets, but there was no scientific evidence to back up the reality of the model.

Greek astronomers also noticed that Mars and Venus varied in brightness. But they could find no explanation for that.

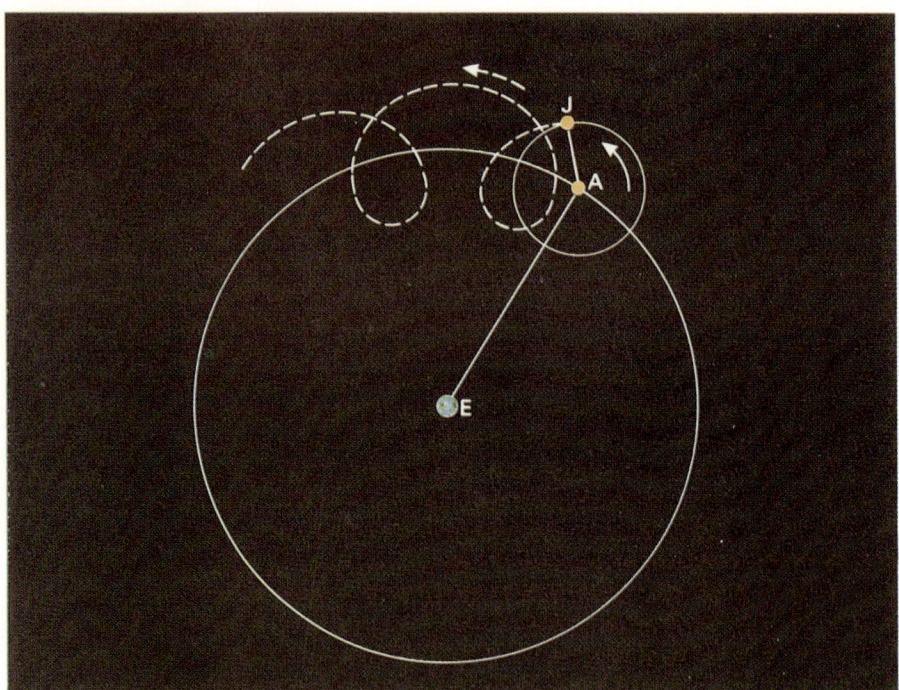

Figure 3
Ptolemy explained the loops of planets with this construction of 'epicycles'

Nicholas Copernicus (1473–1543)

Nicholas Copernicus was a scholarly Polish monk. He divided his time between church duties and studying astronomy. He believed that the universe was a divine creation, but he thought that God's arrangement of the planets would be a simple one.

Copernicus took a bold step, against the teaching of the previous 2000 years. He produced a new model, with a stationary Sun placed at the centre. The Earth and other planets rotate around the Sun. Copernicus explained the motion of the Moon by saying it rotates around the Earth. The daily motion of the stars is explained by the Earth rotating on its axis every 24 hours. It is the Earth that spins round, not the celestial sphere of stars.

Copernicus also measured carefully the planets' orbits. He worked out that Mercury and Venus move in orbits closer to the Sun than the Earth; Mars, Jupiter and Saturn are farther away from the Sun. This theory was very simple and also produced the following successful explanations.

- Copernicus could explain the looping paths of the planets: a loop is caused by a combination of the Earth moving round the Sun, together with the planet moving in a larger orbit round the Sun (Figure 4).

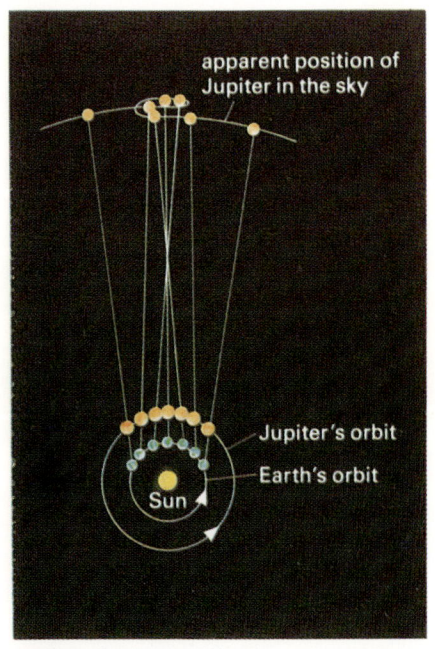

Figure 4
Over a year, Jupiter appears to move through the star pattern. As the Earth overtakes Jupiter, it seems to go backwards

- With the new theory, it was possible to explain why Mars and Venus change in brightness. In Figure 5, Mars appears brighter when it is close to us in position M_1, but duller when it is further away in position M_2.

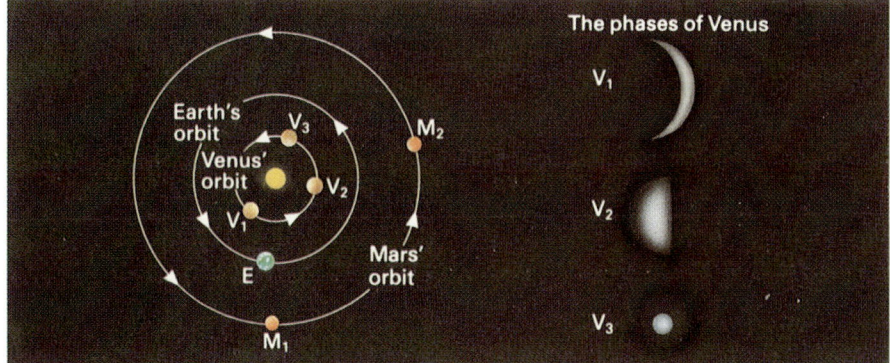

Figure 5
This is how Copernicus thought Mars, Earth and Venus orbited the Sun. The shapes to the right of the diagram show the phases of Venus at positions V_1, V_2 and V_3, when viewed from E

- Copernicus also predicted that, if our eyesight were better, we should see phases of Venus and Mercury just as we can see the Moon's phases.

Galileo Galilei

In 1610, Galileo used the new invention of a telescope to look at the skies. By projecting an image of the Sun, he discovered **sunspots**. He also saw craters on the Moon and rings around Saturn. He looked at Venus over a period of time, and saw the phases that Copernicus predicted.

When Galileo turned his telescope towards Jupiter, he saw what looked like stars close to it. But each night the number and position of the 'stars' changed (Figure 6).

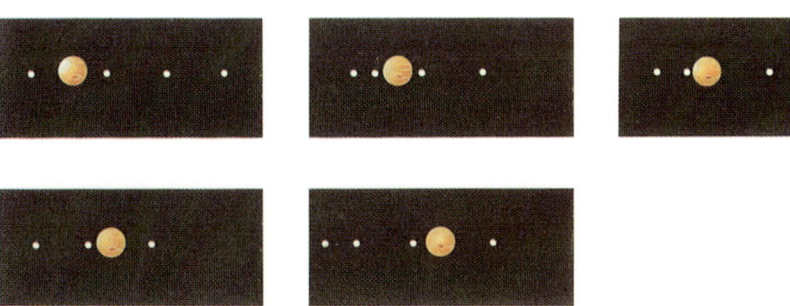

Figure 6
This is how the moons of Jupiter move over a series of nights. On some nights, a moon has disappeared behind Jupiter

He realised that he was seeing four moons in orbit around Jupiter. He could observe their movement over a few hours. This was a miniature solar system that he could see. Jupiter stood in the middle as moons went round it, just as planets rotate about a stationary Sun.

Galileo became a champion of the Copernicus system. He became an outspoken critic of the church's teaching because the church maintained that the Earth and the human race were the centre of God's creation. Eventually, fearing torture or execution, Galileo promised to stop teaching or believing the idea that the Sun stood still.

Venus has a dense atmosphere of carbon dioxide and sulphuric acid, through which it is impossible to see. However, information about its surface has been gathered using radar

QUESTIONS

1 We now believe Copernicus' model of the solar system and not the early Greek model. What did Copernicus manage to explain that the Greeks did not?

2 How did Galileo's observations support Copernicus?

3 (a) 'Facts come first, then theories.' Discuss how this statement applies to the work of (i) Pythagoras, (ii) Copernicus.
(b) Think of another scientific theory. Was the theory based on experimental observations, or did the theory come first?

19 ORIGINS

Michelangelo's Creation of Adam was painted in about 1510. How do our views about the creation of the human race differ from those painted by Michelangelo?

Most of us at an early age start asking questions like 'Where did I come from?' And, when we know the answer to that question, we ask 'Who made the Earth?' This second question is one that has puzzled the human race since the earliest days of civilisation. The ancient Greeks and Romans believed that the Earth was made by three gods: Aether (light), Hemera (day) and Eros (love). Most modern religions have similar creation stories: at some moment in the past a divine being created the Earth, Sun, Moon and stars. Animals and, later, humans were put on the Earth. According to the account in the Book of Genesis in the Bible, this took six days. Modern science too has a story of creation to tell, but it stretches over 15 000 million years.

The galaxy is found in this constellation	Distance of galaxy (millions of light years*)	Speed of galaxy (km/s)
Virgo	72	1200
Perseus	400	
Ursa Major	900	15 000
Corona Borealis	1200	20 000
Bootes	2400	40 000
Hydra		60 000

*1 light year = 10 million million (10^{13}) km. This is the distance light travels in one year.
Table 1

The Big Bang

By 1930, astronomers realised that our Sun is part of an enormous galaxy of stars. They also discovered that there are millions of other galaxies in the universe. By looking carefully at the light sent out by galaxies, Edwin Hubble (1889–1953) worked out that the other galaxies are moving away from us. Table 1 shows the distance of galaxies in various constellations and their calculated speeds.

A small group of galaxies. A computer has colour coded the picture to highlight their speeds. The red galaxies are moving away from us faster than the blue galaxies

Hubble's data suggest that the speed of a galaxy is proportional to its distance away from us (Figure 1). The galaxies in Bootes are twice as far away as those in Corona Borealis; the speed of a galaxy in Bootes is twice as fast as the speed of a galaxy in Corona Borealis. From this law, Hubble could make predictions. By extending the graph (extrapolation) he calculated the distance of far off galaxies; for example, Hydra's measured speed is 60 000 km/s, so it must be about 3600 million light years away.

Hubble's work led to an amazing result. In all directions, galaxies are flying away from us; the further away they are, the faster they go. Billions of years ago, the galaxies must have been a lot closer together. Even further back in time, all the galaxies were in the same place. This led to the idea that the universe originated with an enormous cosmic explosion – the **Big Bang**. About 15 000 million years ago, all of the matter in the visible universe exploded out of a point smaller than a pin head. Physicists call this point a **singularity**. Ever since, matter has been flying outwards away from the explosion.

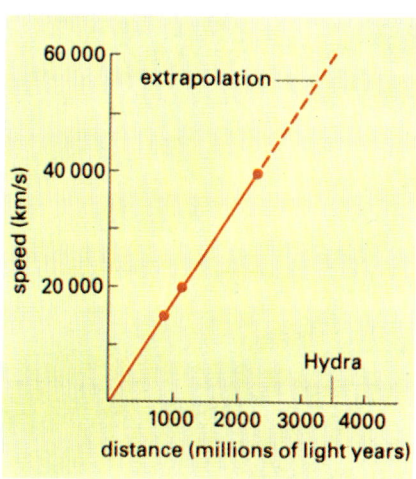

Figure 1
The speed of galaxies is proportional to their distance away from us, according to Hubble's results

Cosmology

Cosmology is the science which tries to explain the origins of the universe. There have been many cosmic theories, but the one most scientists now believe is the Big Bang theory. Minutes after the big bang, the universe was full of only the elementary particles that make up our atoms: electrons, protons and neutrons, together with a lot of radiation. After millions of years (Figure 2), gravity started pulling matter together into large clumps. After a billion (1000 million) years, galaxies were forming. In these galaxies stars began to form. About 10 billion years after the big bang, our Sun and Earth were formed from the remnants of a supernova explosion. In the next 4½ billion years life evolved on the Earth. Eventually, 50 000 years ago, modern man and woman arrived.

Cosmologists have suggested what our universe might have been like right back to the dawn of time. But nobody can explain why there was a big bang. The whole universe was made in an instant, which is even more amazing than other creation stories. Cosmology has neither proved nor disproved the existence of God; the ultimate mystery remains unsolved. Where did the universe come from?

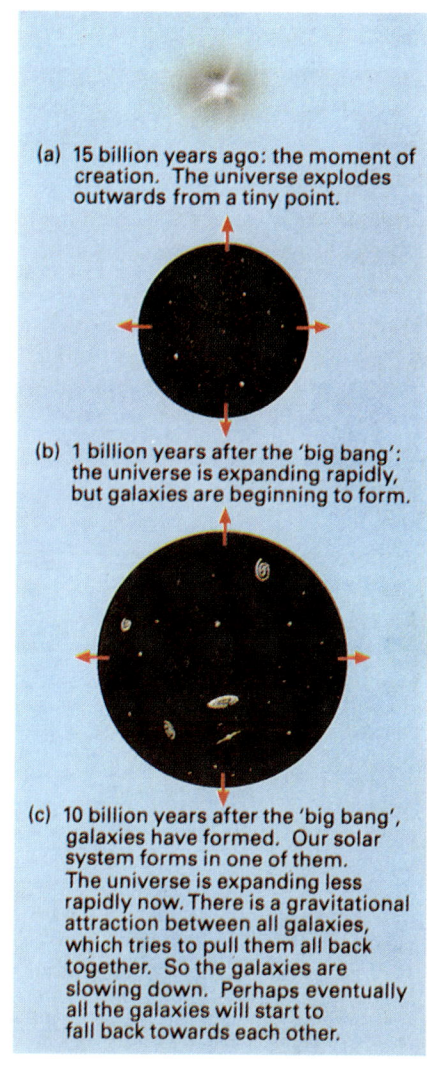

Figure 2

QUESTIONS

1 (a) Look at Table 1. Work out the speed of the galaxies in Perseus.
(b) Quasars are some of the brightest, but most distant objects in the universe. They are very small, but hundreds of times brighter than a galaxy. They are thought to be galaxies which are forming. But we see them as they were a long time ago, because they are so distant.

Such a quasar travels away from us at 200 000 km/s. How far away is it?
2 Explain briefly the evidence for the Big Bang theory.
3 Galaxies are moving away from us, but they are slowing down. Explain why.
4 Darwin's theory of evolution (1859) and modern cosmology have changed our views on creation. Compare modern views on creation with those held by the Romans 2000 years ago.

THINGS TO DO

Study questions – Earth and Atmosphere

1 Make a simple copy of the map below. On it label the winds with the direction from which they come. For each wind, use an atlas to find out what areas they blow over and from which air mass they originate. Explain why the winds are labelled 'good', 'fairly good', 'fairly poor' and 'very bad'.

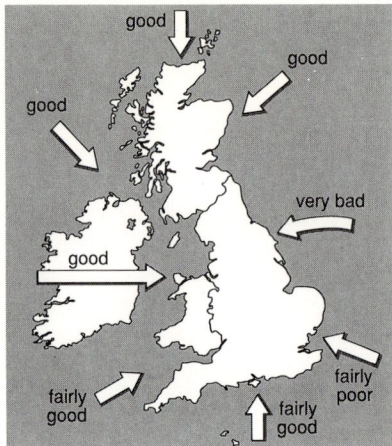

2 What are the main sources of carbon dioxide in the atmosphere? What is the role of carbon dioxide in the atmosphere? What could happen if atmospheric levels of carbon dioxide changed significantly?

3 What is the significance of ozone in the atmosphere? What is causing the amount of ozone to change? What may be the long term consequences of increasing or decreasing the amount of ozone in the atmosphere?

4 The table below shows how incoming radiation is absorbed or reflected by the Earth and its atmosphere. The values are percentages of the total radiation at the outside boundary of the Earth's atmosphere.

Absorption/reflection of radiation	Percentage of total radiation
Reflections from clouds to space	21%
Absorption by clouds	3%
Diffuse reflection to space by dust etc.	5%
Absorption by air molecules (CO_2, O_3, H_2O) and dust	15%
Reflection to space from the Earth's surface	6%

(a) What is the total percentage of incoming radiation reflected by the atmosphere?
(b) What is the total percentage of incoming radiation absorbed by the atmosphere?
(c) What percentage of incoming radiation is transmitted to the Earth's surface?
(d) What percentage of incoming radiation is actually absorbed by the Earth's surface?
(e) What percentage of incoming radiation is lost back to space by reflection by the Earth *and* the atmosphere?

5 The table below shows the major *natural* reservoirs for water on the Earth. The volume of water in each of these reservoirs is given in cubic metres.

Natural reservoir	Volume of water held in reservoir/m^3
Oceans	1350×10^{15} m^3
Glaciers and polar ice	29×10^{15} m^3
Underground water in rocks and natural wells	8.4×10^{15} m^3
Lakes and rivers	0.2×10^{15} m^3
The atmosphere	0.013×10^{15} m^3
The biosphere	0.0006×10^{15} m^3

(a) Calculate the amounts of water held by the oceans as a percentage of the total water in natural reservoirs.
(b) What percentage of the total in natural reservoirs is found as glaciers and polar ice?
(c) How much water is held in the atmosphere as a percentage of all *non-ocean* water?

6 An **aquifer** is a rock which holds water. An **aquiclude** is a rock which will not hold water. An **artesian basin** is a region where water is trapped in an aquifer, often far below the surface. London had a plentiful supply of underground water before it had such a large population. Using the geological cross-section of the London Basin, explain why London had such a good water supply.

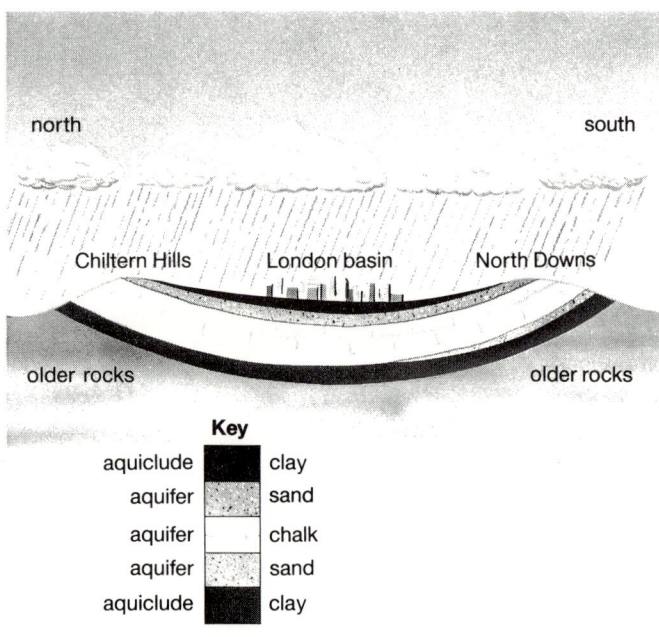

7 Households today use on average 70% more water than households 30 years ago. This is mainly because we now have more household appliances that use water. The table below shows the average amounts of water used by a household.

Use the figures in the table to answer the following questions.

(a) Estimate your own daily consumption.

(b) Estimate your own weekly consumption.

(c) Estimate your own annual consumption.

(d) Now answer (a), (b) and (c) for the other members of your family.

(e) Construct a bar graph to show the amounts of water you use for each purpose.

(f) How could you reduce the amount of water you use?

Reason for water consumption	Average amount of water used at one time/litres
PERSONAL WASHING	
Wash basin	1–3
Bath	70
Shower	25
Power shower	50 (per minute)
LAVATORY	
Old lavatory (before 1989)	7.6
New lavatory (1989 onwards)	6.8
DRINKING AND COOKING	2.5 (per day)
WASHING CLOTHES	
Hand washing	40
Machine washing	80
DISH WASHING	
Hand washing	5
Dishwasher	30
CAR WASHING	
Power spray	40
Bucket	7
WATERING GARDEN	
Sprinkler	800 (per hour)
Watering can	7
LEAKING TAP	
Fast drip (1 drip/second)	100 (per day)
Slow drip (1 drip/10 seconds)	10 (per day)

8 The diagram below shows an alpine area. Make a simple copy of the diagram. By each label line, put the appropriate letter(s) as follows: 'W' for weathering, 'E' for erosion, 'T' for transport, 'D' for deposition. If you know the names of the features shown, you can add these to your diagram too.

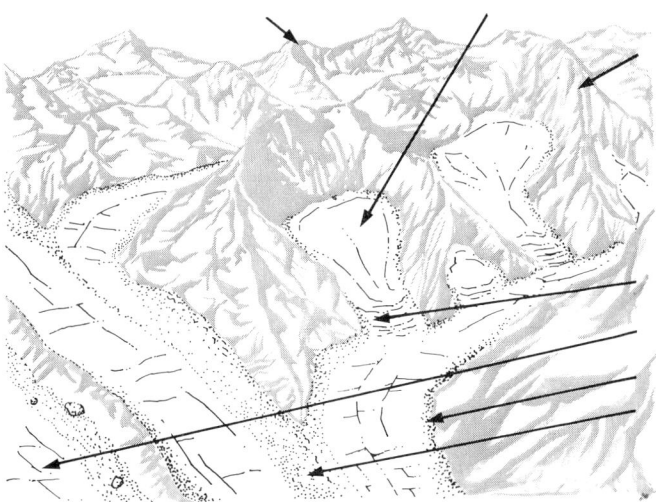

9 The following diagram shows three samples of rock material. They are the same rock type and have an equal volume. Calculate the total surface area for each sample. Which sample would be most susceptible to weathering processes? How will their rates of weathering compare?

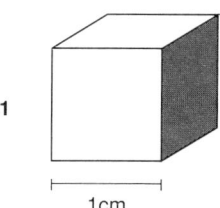

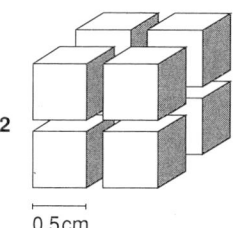

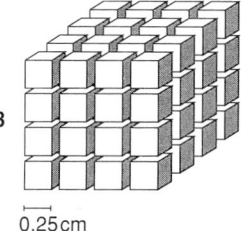

50 THINGS TO DO

10 The table shows data obtained by school children doing a weathering project in a graveyard.

Dates on gravestones	Type of rock		
	Sandstone	Marble	Igneous
1720–1770	extremely badly weathered	very badly weathered	moderately weathered
1771–1819	very badly weathered	badly weathered	moderately weathered
1820–1870	badly weathered	moderately weathered	slightly weathered
1871–1919	moderately weathered	slightly weathered	unweathered
1920–1970	slightly weathered	unweathered	unweathered
1971–1991	unweathered	unweathered	unweathered

(a) Why do you think they chose a graveyard for this study?
(b) What do the results show?

11 The graph below shows the velocity of flow of a stream of water needed to pick up and *transport* particles of different sizes (Curve A). Curve B of the graph shows the velocity of flow at which particles of different sizes come out of suspension and are *deposited*. Use the graph to answer the following questions.

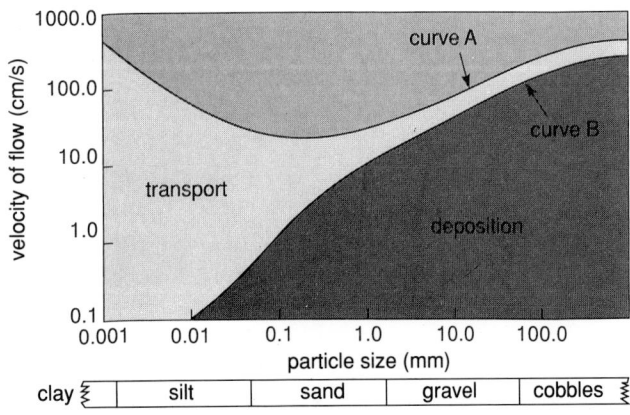

(a) Which type of material is most easily transported?
(b) At approximately what velocity will clay particles be picked up?
(c) At approximately what velocity will coarse gravel be picked up?
(d) In a stream flowing at a velocity below 50 cm per second, what type of material is most likely to be picked up?
(e) Explain the shape of Curve B.

12 The map below shows the location of three seismological stations which record earthquakes. The time that each station receives information on its equipment depends upon its distance from the epicentre of the earthquake. P waves arrive at stations faster than S waves; the time between the arrival of the two types of wave can help the stations to locate the epicentre. The table shows how far each station is from the epicentre.

Continent	Distance of station from epicentre/km	
	Quake 1	Quake 2
A	2500	1800
B	2000	1500
C	1100	3200

(a) Trace the map accurately and, using a compass, construct arcs to locate each epicentre.
(b) Why is it essential to know three distances?
(c) Why do stations receive little data for some earthquakes?

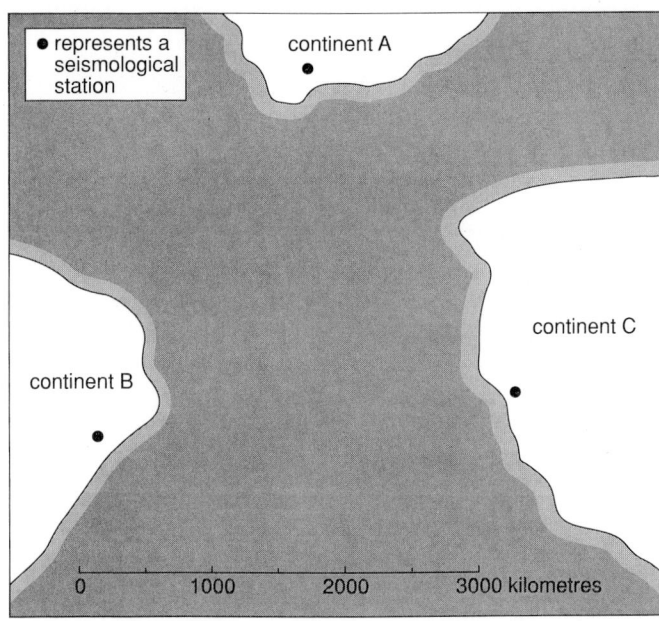

13 The map shows how geologists believe the world might look in eight million years time. What major changes have taken place? What evidence has led geologists to predict these changes?

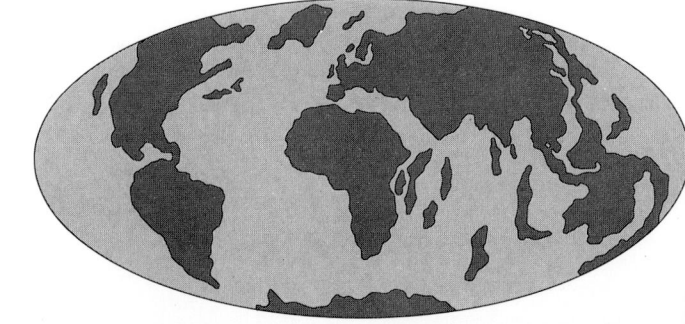

Study questions – Earth and Space

1 As the Moon moves round us, we see it close to different stars each night. The diagrams show the view from Shakila's bedroom window on two consecutive nights in December. On the first night, the moon is near the Pleiades. On the second night, the moon has moved into the constellation of Gemini.

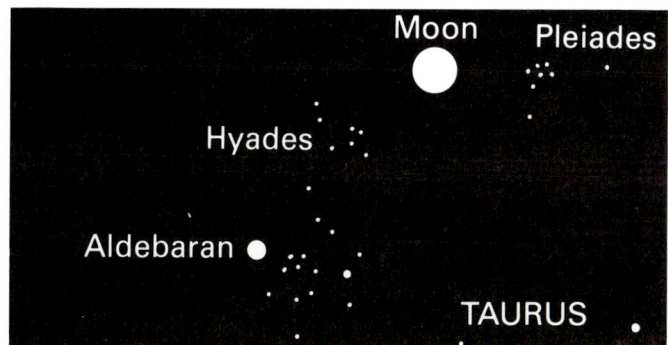

View from Shakila's window on 5 December at 11 pm

View from Shakila's window on 6 December at 11 pm

(a) Draw a diagram to explain why Shakila saw the moon in different positions each night.
(b) Sketch a copy of the stars Shakila saw and show where she saw the moon on 7 December.
(c) Look at the following diagram. Explain where Shakila sees the moon when she gets up on the morning of 12 December.

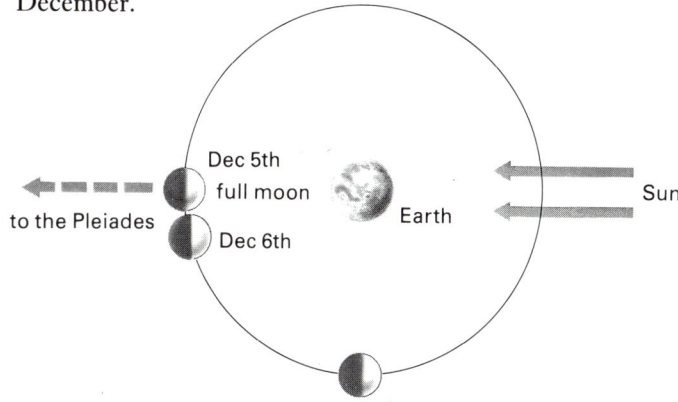

2 Barnard's Star is one of the closest stars to us, at a distance of 6 light years. Careful observation of this star (over some years) shows that it wobbles. The wobble can be explained by the presence of two large planets, which exert a gravitational pull on the star. It is also thought that Vega, a young star, might have planets too. At the moment, very little information has been gathered about other solar systems because Earth-based telescopes have not been able to see planets. It is hoped that, in the future, the Hubble space telescope might show us planets near other stars. Table 1 provides some hypothetical information about planets and their stars, gathered by such a telescope. In this question you are asked to speculate about the conditions on these planets. You might find Table 2 and sections C1 and C8 helpful.

Star name	Star luminosity (Sun = 1)	Star temperature (K)	Star mass (Sun = 1)	Estimated age of star system (millions of years)	PLANET 1		PLANET 2		PLANET 3	
					Mass (Earth = 1)	Distance from star (A.U.)*	Mass (Earth = 1)	Distance from star (A.U.)	Mass (Earth = 1)	Distance from star (A.U.)
Barnard's Star	0.0004	2800	0.1	14 000	80	4	150	7	unknown	unknown
Ophiuchi A	0.5	4900	0.9	10 000	unknown	1	3	2	100	8
Alpha Centauri	1.1	5750	1.1	5000	3	2.5	20	5	70	12
Allenby 247	2.1	5900	1.2	4000	2	1.5	150	7	20	30
Procyon	5.2	6300	1.2	4000	4	2	2	3	15	25
Vega	40	10 600	3	500	5	1	10	6	200	40

*A.U. = 1 Astronomical unit = Earth–Sun distance

Table 1

52 THINGS TO DO

Planet	Distance from Sun (A.U.)	Temperature in day (°C)
Mercury	0.4	350
Earth	1	20
Jupiter	5	−150
Neptune	30	−240

Table 2 *The solar system*

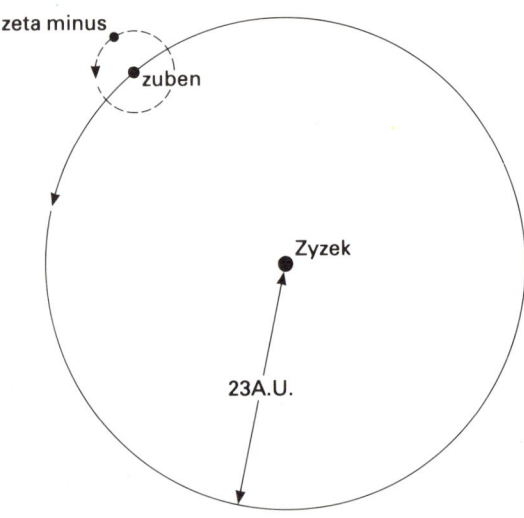

(a) How could an alien astronomer, looking at our Sun, detect that it has a solar system. How long would it take this astronomer to be sure?
(b) Why will a telescope on a spacecraft be better than one of the same size on Earth?
(c) Assuming that other solar systems might be similar to ours, suggest which planets in Table 1 might be rocky and which might contain a large proportion of ice and gas (see unit C8).
(d) Describe what conditions might be like on the surfaces of (i) Vega's innermost planet, and (ii) Barnard's Star's outer planet.
(e) The relative heating effects of stars on the surfaces of planets can be compared using the formula: $H = L/R^2$, where H is the average energy arriving each second on 1 m² of a planet's surface, L is the luminosity of the star, and R is the distance between star and planet in A.U. For example, for the Earth, $L = 1$, $R = 1$, and so $H = 1$.
  Show that H is 1/8 for the second planet of Ophiuchi A. (This means that this planet will be a lot colder than the Earth.)
(f) Use the idea in part (e) to investigate which planet will be nearest to the Earth's temperature and which planet will be nearest to Jupiter's temperature.
(g) Which star system is most likely to support intelligent life? Explain your answer.

3 The (imaginary) planet Zeta minus rotates around its star Zuben. Zeta Minus is a twin planet of the Earth, and Zuben is a star just like our Sun. Use the data and the diagram to answer these questions.

Data
- 1 A.U. = Earth–Sun distance
- Zyzek–Zuben distance = 23 A.U.
- Zuben–Zeta Minus distance = 1 A.U.
- Day length on Zuben = 24 hrs
- Zeta Minus rotates around Zuben once a year
- Zuben rotates round Zyzek once every 43 years
- Zyzek is 25 times brighter than Zuben (as seen from Earth)
- Zeta Minus on average receives 5% of its energy from Zyzek and 95% from Zuben
- Zyzek is 4 times as massive as Zuben

(a) Zyzek is 25 times brighter than Zuben, yet Zyzek provides Zeta Minus with a lot less energy. Explain why.
(b) On average the inhabitants of Zeta Minus live about 120 years. Describe the variations in season and climate that they experience over their lifetime.
(c) In the Zetean language, there are two words for 'night'. The words have a slightly different meaning. Explain what these meanings are.
(d) Zyzek and Zuben are about 50 light years from Earth. Make a sketch to show the observed motion of the two stars over a period of 43 years.

4 Our Moon orbits around us about once every four weeks. Imagine that we had a second smaller moon, in a closer orbit, which goes round us once in two weeks. Describe what sort of tides we would get. Assume that the second moon has the same tidal effect as the Sun (which is about half that of the Moon).

5 Examine carefully the photograph of the moon below. Suggest an explanation, in terms of geological activity, for the features you can see.

6 Kepler's third law of planetary motion states that:

$$\frac{R^3}{T^2} = \text{constant}$$

R is the average distance between the centres of the Sun and the planet, T is the time taken for the planet to orbit the Sun.
(a) The table shows some data for the moons of Uranus. Investigate whether Kepler's third law also holds for a system of moons in orbit round a planet.
(b) Predict the time taken for Oberon to orbit Uranus.

Moons of Uranus

Moon	Average distance of moon from Uranus (1000s of km)	Time for one complete orbit (hours)
Miranda	130	34
Ariel	190	60
Umbriel	270	101
Titania	440	210
Oberon	580	

7 Over the last million years, it is thought that there have been five Ice Ages. These have been dated by geologists. Diagram (1) shows the calculated variation in the Earth's

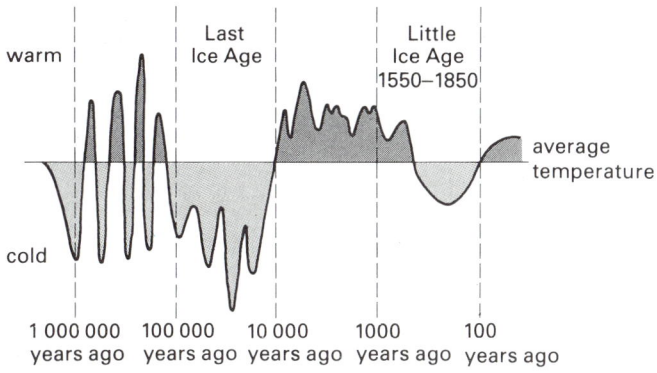

Diagram (1)

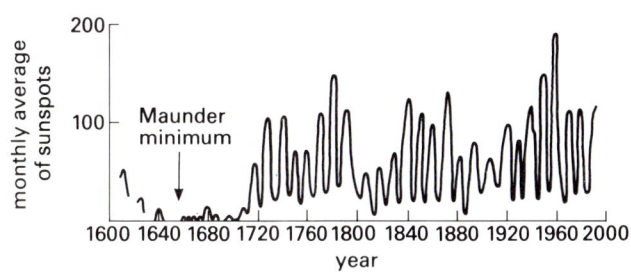

This graph shows the changes in sunspots observed over the last four centuries

Diagram (2)

temperature over this time. This question asks you to consider some theories for the cause of Ice Ages.

Diagram (2) shows the fluctuation in the number of sunspots observed since 1610. Sunspot activity can be seen to vary in a regular cycle. It is possible that the Sun is a little hotter when there are lots of spots. This has little effect on our climate over a short period. However, it is suggested that the absence of spots over a long period might cause the Earth to cool. In diagram (2), you can see a period of about 100 years, 'the **Maunder minimum**', when few observations of sunspots were recorded.
(a) Use diagram (2) to calculate the average period of the sunspot cycle.
(b) Is there enough evidence to link the little Ice Age with a decrease in solar activity? (During the little Ice Age the Earth suffered very severe winters; people were able to skate on the Thames regularly.)
(c) Do you think it is reasonable to link the main Ice Ages with a decrease in solar activity?
(d) Other theories for Ice Ages include these.

- Volcanic eruptions have filled the atmosphere with dust.
- As the Sun rotates around the galaxy, it occasionally passes through regions of dust and gas.
- Variations in the Earth's tilt and orbit have caused cooling.
- Meteorite collisions with the Earth.

Comment on each of these theories, explaining how each might account for the Ice Ages.

ACTIVITIES

Activity 1 A river's load – its transport and deposition

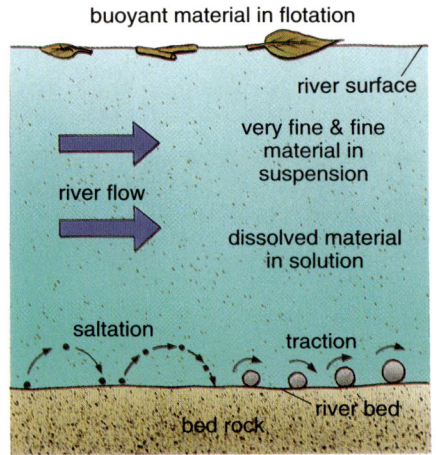

Figure 1
Methods of river transport

Figure 2
Apparatus for river activity

River water has to flow at a certain velocity for particles resting on the river bed to become picked up and then transported. Question 11 in the 'Things to do – Earth and Atmosphere' section shows a graph of critical velocities at which particles of specific sizes are lifted and then carried by water.

Some materials transported are so light that they float on or near the surface, whilst some minerals dissolve and are carried in solution. These materials together are known as the river's load.

Figure 1 shows the different ways a river transports its load:– flotation, suspension, solution, saltation (jumping), and traction (rolling). Not all the load in a river channel will be transported under normal conditions because the river's flow is too slow to carry it all. Some lies deposited on the river bed. In times of flood, when there is a greater volume of water in the river and a faster flow or velocity, then more load will be picked up. This can also include large boulders.

Apparatus

Plastic 'sweet' jar of catering size or other LARGE plastic container with a round base and screw top lid.
Sand and gravel mix. (Equal measures of:– pea-shingle, granules or very coarse sand, medium sand, fine sand. ALL WASHED CLEAN.) (No silt or clay should be used as it clouds the water and makes it difficult to see what is happening.)
Some granular or natural salt, and a sprinkling of organic material. (Leaf debris, pine needles, etc.)
Light (optional).
Hand lens.
Ruler.
Clock or watch with second hand.
Newspaper (to protect desk top).

Method

The pea-shingle, sands, salt and organic debris represent the load carried by a river. Pour a mixture of this into the jar to a depth of 4–5 cm. Pour tap water in till the jar is two-thirds full. Screw the lid tightly on the jar and allow the sediment to settle. The jar now represents part of a river. It must be remembered that flow is circular, unlike a normal river (Figure 3).

QUESTIONS

1 With the base of the jar remaining in contact with the desk top, swirl the jar GENTLY in a clockwise direction for 5 seconds. The water should be moving slowly, at a low velocity and therefore with low energy.

(a) What material is picked up and transported by the water?
(b) Can you identify any methods of transportation?
(c) Time how quickly each type is deposited again.

2 In the same way, swirl the jar a little more forceably for 10 seconds. The water should be moving faster, at a higher velocity and with more energy.

(a) What material is entrained and transported this time?
(b) What methods of transportation can you identify?
(c) Time how quickly the load is deposited.

3 Swirl the jar very forceably for 15 seconds so that all the load is entrained and transported.

(a) What do you notice? Could you hear the sound of particles knocking?
(b) What are these processes? What physical action do they have on a river channel?
(c) Time how long the load takes to settle on the base of the jar.
(d) When it has completely settled, examine the load through the jar, with a hand lens. What grain size can you see at the bottom? What grain size can you see at the top? Explain what you can see.
(e) Is the thickness of the deposited sediment even? If it is thicker in any part of the jar, can you explain why this is?
(f) Without disturbing the sediment, pipette some water from the jar and put it into an evaporating dish. Evaporate the water by heating gently over a Bunsen burner. Examine the residue left with a hand lens. Can you see tiny salt crystals?
4 If you can see any very fine material still in suspension in the water, leave the jar still for several hours. Examine the sediment with a hand lens again when the water is clear. What does this tell you about the transport of silt and clay particles?

Figure 3
The jar is a circular river

Activity 2   Folded sediments and geological patterns

Sedimentary beds are always deposited with the oldest beds at the bottom and the youngest at the top. (This is the Law of Superposition.) Generally the beds form horizontal layers. However, with tectonic activity, horizontal beds can become folded. (Folded beds produce, after erosion, a paired banded pattern when mapped or seen from high above. Hard bands of rock form upland and soft bands of rock lowland.)

Folds never continue over vast distances, so the paired bands pattern changes where the beds are less steeply dipping. When beds dip towards each other, a downfold or syncline is produced. Where beds dip away from each other an upfold or anticline is made. Synclines and anticlines are found next to each other.

The sedimentary beds of South East England were folded at the same time that the Alps were forming. Because South East England was at a distance from the main force of folding in Central Europe, the folds are gentle and did not produce high mountains but areas of upland where there were anticlines, and lowland where there were synclines. Erosion since the folds first formed has removed part of each bed, leaving a distinctive pattern of different rock beds exposed at the surface. Harder bands of rock now form higher land, whilst softer bands of rock form lower land. Figure 4 shows the present day pattern of these beds where they outcrop.

Apparatus

Plasticine of three different colours.
Rolling pin or jam jar to roll sheets of Plasticine.
Blunt knife (eg table knife.)

Method

Roll each colour of Plasticine into a rectangular sheet approximately 30 cm × 10 cm × 1.5 cm. Place the different coloured sheets one on top of each other. Trim any uneven edges. Number the beds, 1 at the bottom, 2 in the middle, and 3 at the top. (1 is the oldest bed and 3 the youngest.) (Figure 5a.)
Now using the diagrams as a guide:—
1. Bend one end of the rectangular sheet into a downfold or syncline and the other end into an upfold or anticline. (Figure 5b.) (This is now like the huge upfold and downfold created in South East England during the time that the Alps were forming between 25 million and 7 million years ago.)

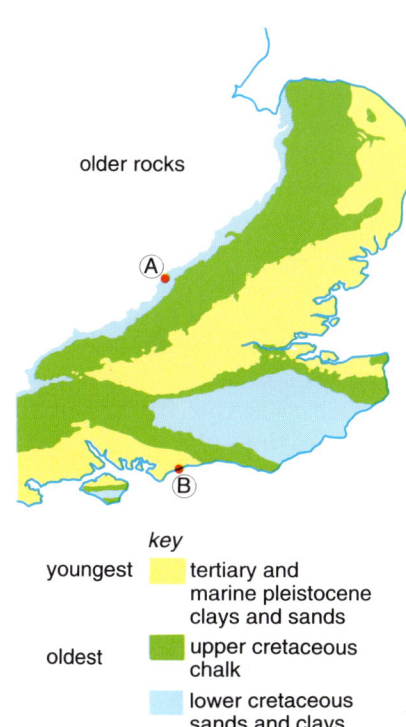

Figure 4
Simple geological map of South East England

QUESTIONS

1 Does the pattern on your model look anything like a pattern you can see on the geological map of South East England? Trace the map and on it draw a rectangle where you can see the same pattern as your model.

2 In your downfold, or syncline, which beds are found in the middle, the oldest or the youngest?

3 In your upfold, or anticline, which beds are found in the middle, the oldest or the youngest?

4 On your tracing of the geological map of South East England draw a line from 'A' in the north to 'B' in the south. The line cuts across layers of rocks of various ages, sometimes crossing the same layers more than twice. With a straight edge of paper accurately mark off the boundary of each different layer you cross from 'A' to 'B'. Bearing in mind what you have already discovered about folds, and the patterns that erosion of folded rock layers create at the surface, complete the section to show the Alpine folds of England's south east corner. Draw solid lines below the section line to show the layers under the surface. Draw dotted lines above the section line to show where the rock layers were before erosion removed them. Colour in your section using the same colours as shown on the map and diagrams.

5 On your completed section, label the anticline, the syncline, and each layer.

6 From which direction did the force which created these Alpine folds come?

2. Cut the Plasticine model completely in two along the line shown in Figure 5b. (This now looks like a section of South East England since erosion, occurring over millions of years, has removed much of the upfold.)

Explanation of procedure

Figure 5a. The layers of Plasticine represent layers of sedimentary rock. The oldest rock beds are at the bottom and the youngest are at the top. These beds have not been changed by tectonic forces into folds.

Figure 5b. The once horizontal beds have been pushed up into a huge upfold or anticline with a corresponding downfold or syncline, just like the folds in South East England which formed between 25 million and 7 million years ago.

Figure 5c. Cutting the top off the anticline and slicing through part of the syncline represents the effects of erosion. Over millions of years, since South East England formed, erosion has removed most rock material from the high upfolded area and less from the low downfolded area.

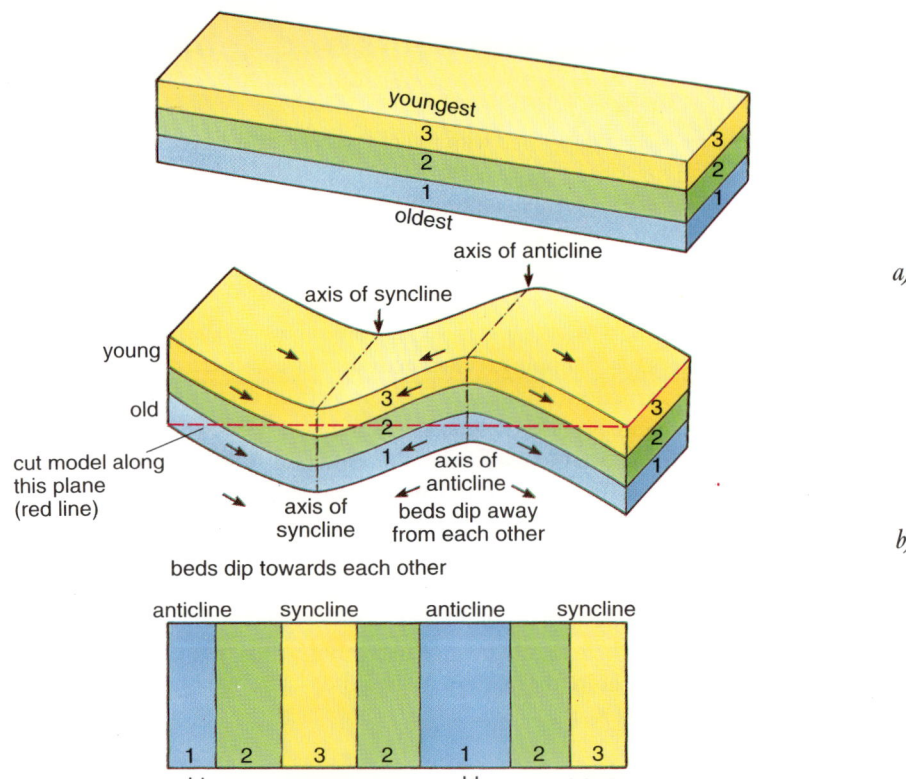

Figure 5 Procedure for making the Plasticine model

Activity 3 Continental drift in the classroom

In this activity you will create a model to help you understand continental break-up, sea floor spreading, subduction and the creation of fold mountains. Your model can also be used to demonstrate continental collision, the final stage of the tectonic cycle.

Apparatus

Four school desks or tables to represent the earth's surface.
Two 'continents' made from box lids, polystyrene or wood. (These should be less than half the size of one desk top ideally.)

EARTH AND SPACE 57

'Ocean floor' made from paper, the total length of the four desks.
'Sediments' made from coloured tissue paper.
Cone bases cut out from egg boxes to represent volcanic islands.
Crayons and ruler to draw 'paired magnetic bands' on the new 'ocean floor'.
You should work in groups of two to four. You might find it useful to refer to Figure 2 in section 8 of this book as you work.

Explanation of the apparatus used in this tectonic model

The four desks represent part of the Earth's surface. The gap between the middle two desks represents the point at which hot mantle material domes the surface and creates a rift valley. This gap becomes the ocean ridge where new oceanic crust is created. As the rift valley opens to form a linear sea, and then a wider ocean, the gaps between the inner two desks and the outer two desks will become ocean trenches – the subduction zones where ocean crust is pushed down and destroyed. The box lids represent the lighter, thicker, continental material which rides on top of the denser, thinner oceanic crust, represented by the length of paper. As the ocean widens, sediments build up on the ocean floor and in the shallower part of the ocean against the edge of the continent which is known as the continental shelf. Sheets of coloured tissue paper represent the layers of sediment that accumulate. Small cones cut from egg boxes can be used to represent island arc volcanoes.

Method

Follow the diagrams showing six tectonic stages, from above and from the side.

Diagram 1. THE BREAK UP OF A SUPERCONTINENT
(Our continents today were once joined into vast supercontinents which have drifted apart eg. South America and Africa, North America and Eurasia.) Place the two halves of 'supercontinent AB' (box lids) on top of the two ends of the 'ocean floor' (length of paper folded in half lengthways and fed into the narrow gap between the middle two desks). Secure each end of the paper (oceanic crust) to a box lid (the 'supercontinent'). The model now represents Figure 2a of Section 8.

Diagram 2. THE CREATION OF A LINEAR SEA
Pull the two halves of supercontinent AB apart, so that there is a 'linear sea' about 20 cm between them with the 'rift valley' down the middle. They should be equally spaced. The ocean floor is made of basalt lava which takes on the Earth's polarity at that time. (The Earth's magnetic field reverses from time to time. At the present day it is normal and the magnetic pole is north. In the past the Earth's magnetic field has alternated between being reversed – with the magnetic pole south, or normal.) Using a ruler and coloured pencil, crayon or marker, draw two thick lines on the 'ocean floor', one close to each side of the 'rift valley' gap. Decide whether the Earth's polarity is normal or reversed as this new 'ocean floor' is forming. Colour the 'ocean floor' if it is normal polarity, leave it blank if it is reversed. Now pull each of your continents out by another 10 cm or so. Again draw in two thick lines to show the new bands of 'ocean floor' which have just been created. If your last bands were formed when the Earth's polarity was normal, by now it has become reversed, so leave these bands blank. If the last bands were formed during reversed polarity, the Earth has now reverted to normal polarity – so colour these new bands in. Repeat this whole process twice more. The model now represents Figure 2c of Section 8.

Diagram 3. THE EXPANDING OCEAN
Continue to separate the two continental halves at an equal rate, creating new oceanic crust with paired bands of normal and reverse polarity. Each time you do so, lay tissue paper of the same colour (to represent the same age) next to the continent

Diagram 1

Stage 1. The break up of supercontinent AB.

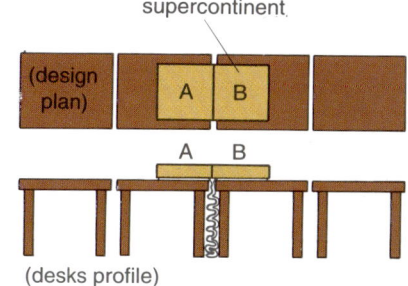

Diagram 2

Stage 2. The creation of a linear sea.

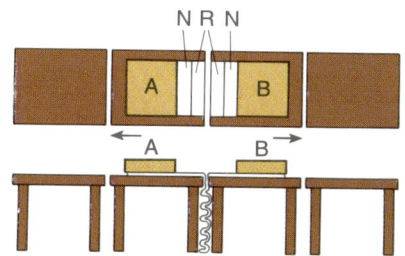

Diagram 3

Stage 3. The expanding ocean.

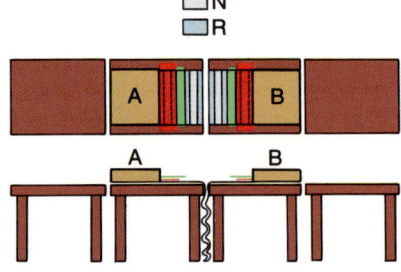

Diagram 4

Stage 4. The still expanding ocean is subducted in the trench.

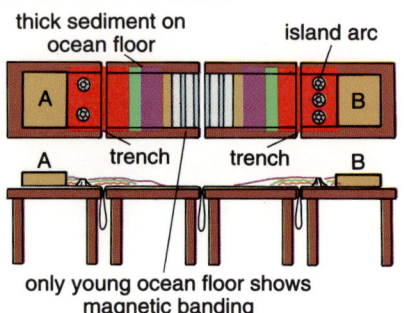

Diagram 5

Stage 5. Mountain building, new continental material is added.

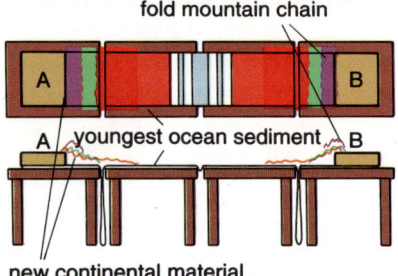

Diagram 6

Stage 6. Continental collison and end of cycle.

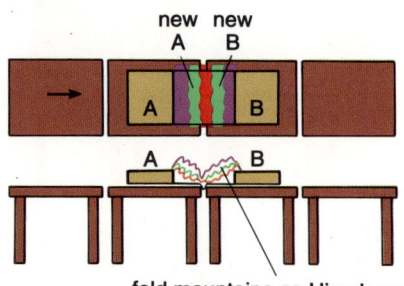

on each side of your 'ocean ridge'. Continue to add a layer to each side each time your ocean expands. You can mark with a coloured crayon submarine volcanoes (which may become volcanic islands on the ridge) and which, as the ocean expands, become long chains of seamounts. Gradually move each continent to the end desk on that side, placing it approximately 20 cm away from the gap between the outer and inner desks. (This border next to the continent represents the shallow sea area of the continental shelf.) The model now represents Figure 2d of Section 8.

Diagram 4. SUBDUCTION IN OCEAN TRENCHES

The continents are now static, but new ocean floor is still being produced. The weight of the sediment which has built up near the continents causes the thin ocean floor to buckle and break. Because it's denser, the ocean floor sinks. We say it is subducted. The layers of lighter sediment on top do not sink and are forced up against the edge of the continent. To simulate this, gently thread the paper (ocean floor) down the gap between the end desks and the inner desks. As you do this, the tissue paper (sediment) crinkles and folds against the edges of continents A and B. On the continent side of the gap (the ocean trench) place two or three cones to represent volcanic islands formed from magma produced as the oceanic plate is pushed down and melts. (These will become incorporated into fold mountains in the next stage.) The model represents Figure 2e of Section 8.

Diagram 5. MOUNTAIN BUILDING

Continue generating new ocean floor at the ocean ridge in the middle exactly as before, adding further layers of tissue 'sediment', until there is no more paper left to make more ocean floor. At the same rate at which this new crust is created the older ocean crust is subducted into the trenches. The tissue 'sediments' will have rucked up into lines of folds which represent a fold mountain chain. At this stage the old ocean may actually be closing up a little as a new ocean opens elsewhere on Earth, and the continents may lie closer to the trenches. Push the box lids to within 10 cm of the 'trenches'. The model now represents Figure 1 of Section 8 in this activity. (The activity can end at this stage or continue to the close of the tectonic cycle.)

Diagram 6. CONTINENTAL COLLISION

Move the two continents slowly towards each other. Lay down further sediment in the sea as you do so. The continents need not move at equal rates, one might even remain static. As they approach the sediments in the closing ocean become pushed up into a thick area of fold mountains forming a join between the two continents.

N.B. In this last stage the model is not strictly accurate. The continents colliding may not be the same ones that separated originally. They may be continents which have never been joined before, but join for the first time as they move towards each other and collide. (eg India and Eurasia.)

Activity 4   Earthquake hazards

In the winter of 1964 Alaska was severely affected by an intense earthquake. The surface waves spreading from the epicentre caused the ground to rise and fall like sea waves, with amplitudes of between three and four feet. Three-foot wide cracks opened and closed in the ground. In places, frozen ground was broken into angular pieces which the earthquake left lying at uneven angles. Landslides were triggered by the shaking and large areas slid into the sea. The landslides created huge water waves which, together with tsunamis (tidal waves) generated at sea by the 'quake, further damaged Alaska's coastal settlements.

EARTH AND SPACE

Areas closest to the epicentre are not necessarily those most damaged by an earthquake. Much depends upon the nature of the rocks. Hard rocks are more resistant to the surface seismic waves. But soft sediments amplify shaking, and buildings constructed upon them suffer more damage than buildings on hard rocks. Soft sediments may also liquify, becoming like quicksand – buildings fall and sink, and buried light objects can rise to the surface. Much depends upon the nature of the sediment particles, how well they are packed and the amount of water they contain in spaces between particles, as well as the intensity of shaking and how long it goes on.

In this activity, you will demonstrate what happens when a soft sediment rock becomes liquified during an earthquake. The activity is a simulation of the effects of the 1964 Alaska earthquake at Valdez. Work in pairs.

Apparatus

A plastic tray or plastic lined box about 25 cm × 40 cm or larger.
Enough clean washed sand to 2/3 fill the tray or box.
Pieces of wood, tile, slate, etc. about the size of a domino or smaller to represent buildings.
A few pieces of polystyrene of a smaller size to represent structures below the surface (eg. septic tanks, coffins.) Newspaper for the box to stand on.
Water.

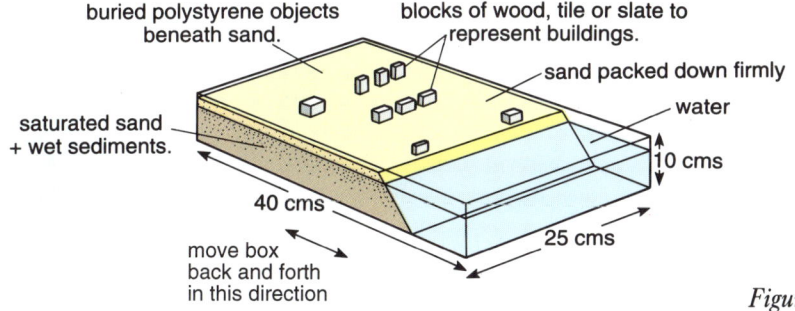

Figure 6
Apparatus for earthquake simulation

Method

Fill the box with sand up to 2/3 its length, and firm down the sand to squeeze out as much air space as possible. The sand should taper down to the base at the empty end. Fill this empty space carefully and slowly with water, trying not to disturb the sand. The water will be taken up by the sand, so add some more when the level drops. Do not add too much. (The sand should look damp but not wet.) Bury polystyrene 'coffins' and 'septic tanks' in the sand and firmly press 'buildings' into

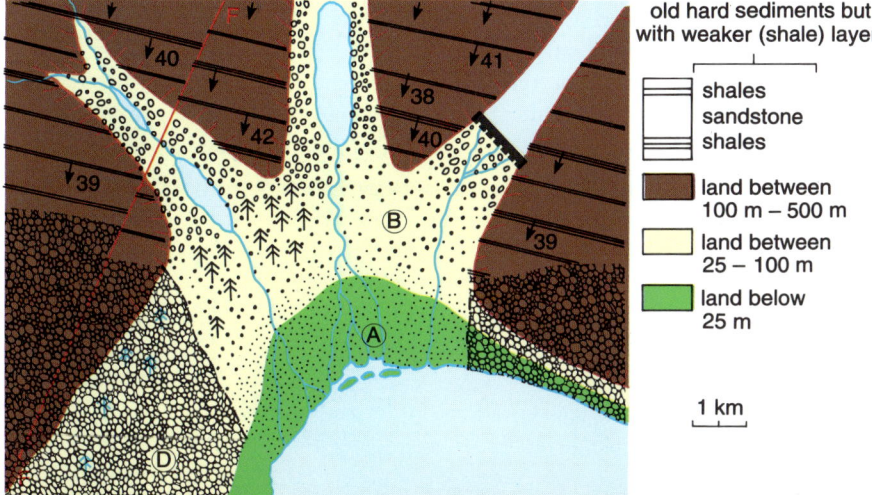

- Break up of ground – land close to active fault
- Ground shaking – Most intense near moving fault, less intense with distance from fault. Soft sediments amplify shaking, hard rock resists it
- Liquefaction – Soft sediments become quicksand
- Landslides – Near hilly or mountainous regions after heavy rain, or where slopes are unstable due to rock type or sparse vegetation
- Flooding – From tsunamis in coastal districts, ponding up of rivers by landslides, failure of dams

QUESTIONS

Study the data about earthquake hazards (above) and the map of an imaginary area subject to earthquakes. Imagine that four possible sites have been surveyed for a new town and that you have to decide on the safest place for it to be built.

- A was chosen because it offers a sheltered harbour for shipping.
- B was chosen because there is plenty of clear low land for the town to develop on.
- C was chosen because it is furthest from the active fault.
- D was chosen because it is on hard rock good for foundations.

1 List for each of the sites A–D the possible earthquake hazards that exist.
2 Choose the site which you think is the safest and explain why you would build the new town there and not at the other sites.

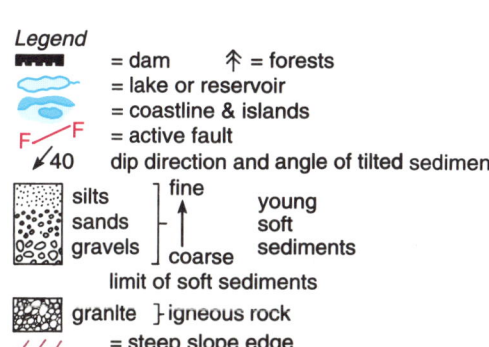

place at the surface (Figure 1). While one person observes, the other should simulate the earthquake, as follows. Keeping the box base in contact with the table shake the box gently at first by moving the box slowly back and forth over a distance of about 5 cm. Increase the rate of shaking gradually. Note what happens to the 'buildings' and the buried objects. Note also what happens at the sand/water edge.

After the earthquake in Alaska in 1964, planners studied the earthquake hazards and decided to rebuild Valdez on harder rocks nearby.

Activity 5 Weathering processes

Weathering is the name given to the processes by which rocks break down in place. All rocks have some particular weakness which makes them vulnerable to one of the many physical, chemical or biological weathering processes.

The factors which affect the rate of weathering are:– climate (which may be:– cold dry, cool wet, warm wet, hot dry), aspect (sunny, shaded, windward, etc.), biota (plants and animals), rock structure (cracks, fissures, porosity, particle size), rock type, and the presence of underground water.

Weathering happens more rapidly in climates where water is readily available. If there are warm seasons, chemical weathering can operate effectively. If there are cold spells when temperatures drop below freezing then the mechanical process of freeze-thaw weathering can take place.

Igneous and metamorphic rocks are made of a mosaic of different mineral crystals locked together. They are very hard rocks and generally more resistant. But not all the minerals can equally withstand weathering processes and if one mineral breaks down faster than the others (eg feldspar which breaks down to kaolin in granites) then the outside of the hard rock becomes rotten and crumbles away.

Sedimentary rocks are made of particles which are compacted and cemented together. Sometimes there are pore spaces between the particles where water can get in. These rocks are porous and permeable. Water may enter the pore spaces and tiny cracks in the rock. In winter, if the temperature drops below freezing after a wet period then the water will turn to ice crystals. When water freezes it expands slightly. Inside the cracks and pore spaces the ice crystals exert a pressure and this begins to force the particles in the rock apart. Eventually the rock is weakened and will break. This is freeze-thaw weathering or gelifraction. In Activity (i) rocks are subjected artificially to this type of weathering.

Rocks which are made of large crystals or particles weather more slowly than rocks made of small crystals or particles. This is because the large crystals/particles have a small surface area compared to their volume, whilst small crystals/particles have a large surface area compared to their volume. This is known as their surface to volume ratio. (It is like the difference between sucking one gobstopper sweet compared with several small sweets of an equal volume. The gobstopper takes longer to dissolve.) Most minerals will not dissolve readily but salt is an example of a mineral which is very soluble. In Activity (ii) it can be used to represent the effect that water can have on soluble minerals – but usually over a much longer time. It also shows that large crystals of the same type are much more resistant than small crystals, and take longer to weather.

(i) Apparatus

Samples of porous rocks eg chalk, 'soft' limestone, sandstone.
Sample of a non-porous rock eg granite.
Sample of piece of porous clay flower pot.
Container – bowl or plastic box.
Scales for weighing.
Hand lens.
Water and deepfreeze.

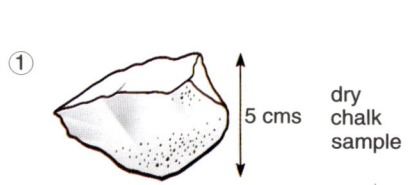

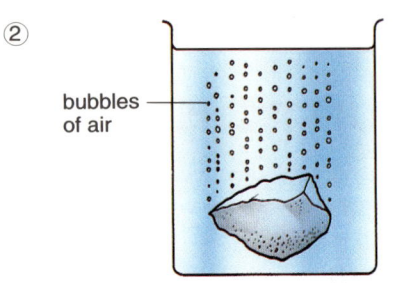

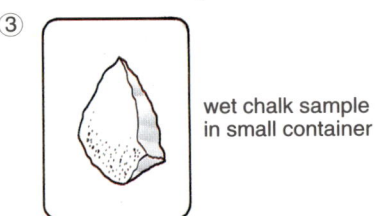

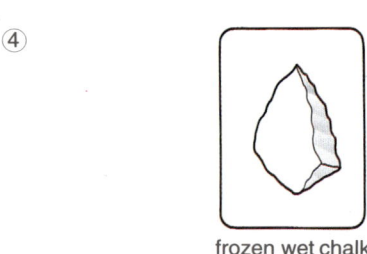

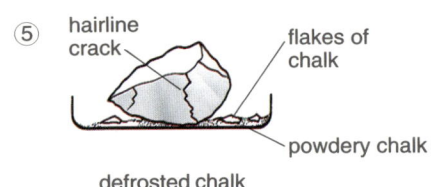

Figure 7
Method for Activity (i)

Method

Take each sample chosen and observe carefully with a hand lens. Can you see any tiny holes or small cracks?

Weigh each rock sample whilst dry. Record the dry weight. Saturate each sample in water – preferably for one hour at least, or overnight. Weigh each sample again. Record the wet weight. If there is a difference in weight then your sample is porous and has taken in water. (Very porous rock samples 'fizz' bubbles of air when immersed in water.) Drain away excess water and place your samples into a deepfreeze overnight or longer.

Remove your 'frozen' samples from the deepfreeze and allow to defrost completely. (This may take some hours.) Examine with a hand lens.
1. Can you see any tiny cracks which weren't visible before?
2. Is the surface of any of the rock samples more crumbly than before? If so, which samples? Have any small pieces dropped off?

Immerse each sample in water again until air bubbles stop rising. Reweigh specimens and repeat the freezing and thawing processes again. After each occasion examine with a hand lens and record any changes observed in the rock samples.
3. Can any of the samples be broken easily by hand? If so, which?
4. Have any of the samples remained totally unchanged? If so, which?
Allow all samples to dry completely, then reweigh.
5. Are any of the rock samples lighter than before? If so, which?
6. Of the different rock samples chosen for this activity, which do you think is the most vulnerable to freeze-thaw weathering? Which do you think is the most resistant? Why do you think this is so?

(ii) Apparatus

One large piece of rock salt crystal, sea salt crystals, table salt.
Scales for weighing.
Hand lens.
Glass beakers.
Clock or watch with second hand.
Stirring rod.
Water.

Method

Take one large crystal of rock salt (about 15–20 g) and weigh accurately. Then weigh out equal amounts to this of sea salt crystals and table salt. Examine each sample with your hand lens.

Place each in a separate glass beaker. Taking the table salt first (the smallest crystals), pour into the beaker 200 cm³ of water. Note the exact time and start stirring vigorously. Stir until all the table salt crystals have dissolved completely, then stop and note the exact time this has taken.

Next pour 200 cm³ of water into the sea salt container and stir vigorously for exactly the same length of time as before, then stop. Examine the sea salt crystals. Do they look any smaller? Has their shape changed? Continue timing and stir until all these crystals have completely dissolved. Note the length of time that this takes.

Next pour 200 cm³ of water onto the rock salt crystal and stir for the same length of time as you did for the table salt. Take out the crystal, examine and weigh it accurately. What do you observe? Place it again in the water and stir for the total length of time that the sea salt took to dissolve. Remove the rock salt crystal, examine and weigh again.

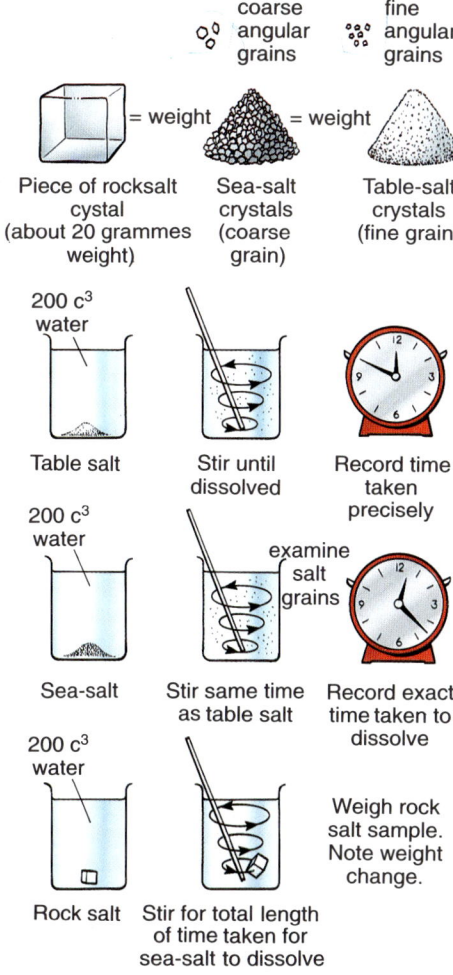

Figure 8 Method for Activity (ii)

QUESTIONS

1 Which salt sample dissolved the fastest and why?
2 What shape were the sea salt crystals to begin with? What shape were they after being partially dissolved? What had happened to their size?
3 Were the corners of the rock salt crystal angular to begin with? What shape were they after being stirred for the same time that the table salt took to dissolve? What weight was the rock salt crystal at this stage?
4 What weight was the rock salt crystal after it had been stirred for the length of time that the sea salt took to dissolve?
5 What does this experiment tell you about the importance of the size of crystals in weathering processes?

QUESTIONS

1 (a) A star has a parallax angle of 1/30 second. How far away is it in:
(i) parsecs, (ii) light years?
(b) A light year is the distance that light will travel in a year. Work out the answer to part (a) in km. (Light travels at a speed of $300\,000$ km/s; there are about 3×10^7 s in a year).

2 The Andromeda Nebula and the Magellanic Clouds are two galaxies which can be seen by eye. Clarissa, an astronomer, knows that the Magellanic Clouds are about 180 000 light years away from us. She does not know how far away the Andromeda Nebula is but she wants to work it out. Below you can see some data she found by looking at some cepheid variables in the two galaxies.
(a) Which galaxy is nearer to us?
(b) Compare cepheids with the same period from the two galaxies. Roughly how many times brighter are the cepheids in the Magellanic Clouds?
(c) What relative brightness does a cepheid of period 0.7 days have in the Andromeda Nebula?
(d) Now use the rule shown in the diagram, and your answer to part (b), to calculate how far the Andromeda Nebula is away from us.

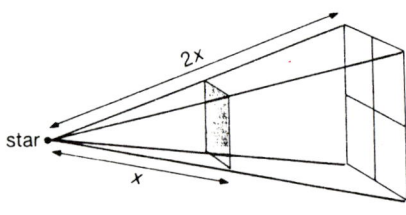

Galaxy	Period of cepheid in days	Relative brightness of cepheid
Andromeda Nebula	1.7	13
	2.4	19
	3.8	30
Magellanic Clouds	0.7	490
	1.7	1280
	3.8	3100
	4.9	4080

Activity 6 Light in the night sky

The article below is about astronomy. Read it carefully and then answer the questions.

Many years ago astronomers were puzzled by strange fuzzy objects that were visible in the night sky. Some of these objects can be seen by eye, others were only visible in their telescopes. They called the objects nebulas; the word nebulous means hazy or indistinct. The nature of the nebulas remained a mystery for a long time because no telescope was powerful enough to show any details of any nebula.

In 1947 the Hale telescope on Mount Palomar was completed. This telescope is the world's largest. Its mirror has a diameter of 5 m. The mirror alone weighs over twenty tonnes. The focal length of the mirror is about 20 m. When astronomers used this telescope to look at nebulas the results were truly amazing. Some of the nebulas turned out to be clouds of gas and stars at distances of only a few hundred light years. But some nebulas were found to be whole galaxies of stars like our own milky way.

Discoveries with the Hale telescope came thick and fast. It is now thought that the universe contains some thousand million (10^9) galaxies. On average each galaxy contains about a hundred thousand million (10^{11}) stars. The furthest galaxies from us are enormous distances away. The Hale telescope has photographed galaxies at distances of 5000 million light years. Light from these galaxies started its journey towards us before the Earth had been formed.

Measuring the distance to stars

When you go for a walk through a wood you will notice that the trees nearest to you appear to move relative to the more distant trees. The same effect happens with stars. Those stars near to us appear to move relative to the more distant stars as we go around the sun. The bigger the apparent movement of the star the closer it is to us. Figure 9 shows how a star near to us makes a different angle with a distant star during the course of a year.

If the parallax angle is 1 second of arc then the star is said to be 1 parsec away. (1 parsec is about 3.3 light years). If the angle is 1/10 of a second of arc then the star is 10 parsecs away. The smaller the angle, the bigger the distance. Parallax angles are very small and hard to measure. Only distances as far as 200 light years or so can be measured by parallax.

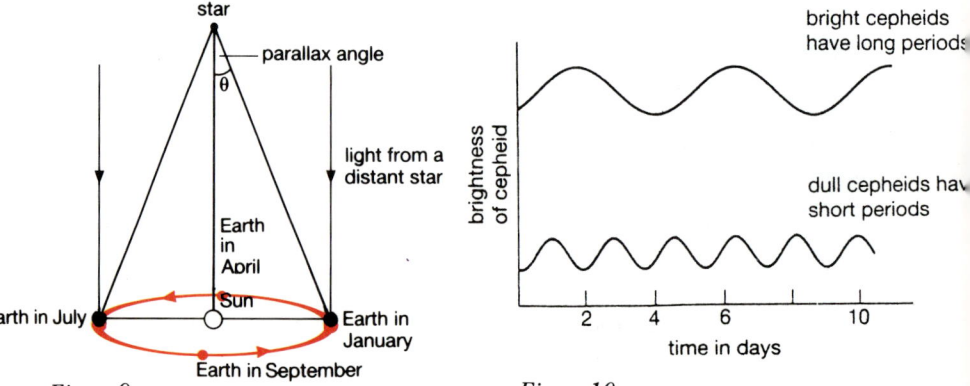

Figure 9

Figure 10

Cepheid variables are stars whose brightness varies over a period of a few days. The bigger and brighter the star is the longer it takes for its brightness to go through one full cycle (Figure 10). The important point is that any two stars, which take the same time for one cycle (3 days for example), are equally bright. So if you see two cepheids with the same *period* but different apparent *brightnesses* you can conclude that the duller one is further away.

Activity 7 Summer stars

It is often said that the best time to view stars is in January. It is true that the most brilliant of constellations (Orion) is visible then, and on a dark, cold, clear night the conditions for observation can be excellent. However, bitter cold can limit the amount of time you are prepared to stay outside. On a summer's night there is something to see and it is more pleasant outside. The best way to view in the summer is lying flat on your back on the ground, or sitting in a deckchair.

Figure 11 shows what you will see overhead at midnight in July. Shown on the star map are four constellations, Cygus, Lyra, Sagitta and Aquila.
1. Go outside on a clear night and identify the four constellations.
2. Find the three bright stars Altair, Vega and Deneb.
3. Add some extra stars that you have seen, to your star map.
4. On a dark, moonless night, you will see a light, white patch running through these constellations. This is also marked on your map; this is the milky way. When you see the milky way, you are looking into our own galaxy. If you have a pair of binoculars you will see that the milky way is rich with magnificent star fields.
5. As a bonus, if you look at this view between August 12th and 14th you will see meteors. Every year at about this time we pass through the Perseid shower. Sometimes you can see a meteor every minute; you see great streaks passing across the sky. If you watch carefully you will also be able to pick out satellites in orbit round the earth (these are of course visible every night of the year).

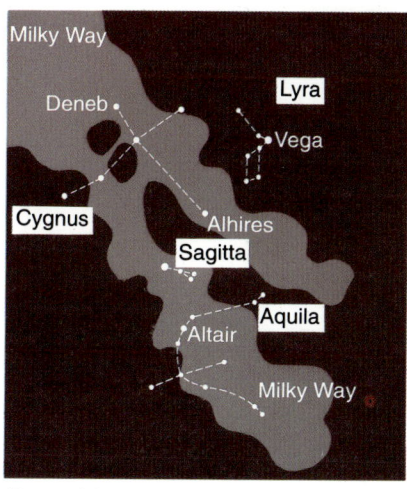

Figure 11

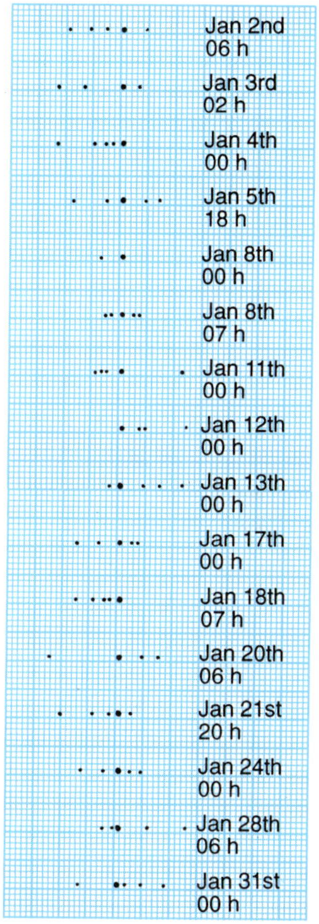

Activity 8 Jupiter's moons

In January 1610 Galileo turned his newly made telescope towards Jupiter. Figure 12 shows the sort of sightings Galileo would have seen (this sequence was actually observed in 1992). Galileo saw Jupiter with what looked like four 'stars' next to it. But each night that he looked the position and number of these 'stars' varied. He realised that he was watching moons move around Jupiter; some nights the moons cross in front of the planet or go behind so we see less than four. The moons move around in roughly circular orbits. However, we do not see these circular paths because we look at their motion from sideways on. So the moons appear to move backwards and forwards in a straight line.

By careful observation, it is possible to work out which moon is which, together with the size of the radius of a moon's orbit, and the time taken to orbit. For example, Europa reaches its furthest point west on January 18th 0700h and again on 21st 2000h. It is then about four and a half 'squares' from the centre of the planet.

Such a grid can be put onto the eyepiece of a telescope to help the observer take measurements. Here one square has the same size as Jupiter's diameter. So we can say that Europa's orbit is four and a half Jupiter diameters. The time of orbit is 3 days 13h or about three and a half days.

Use the observations and Figure 12 to help you fill in the gaps on the table and answer the questions.

Figure 12

QUESTIONS

1 Which moon is moving most quickly?
2 Which moon is moving most slowly?
3 Why did we see only one moon on January 8th 0000h?
4 For the observations taken on January 31st, work out which moon is which and put the names on the diagram.

Moon	Radius of orbit (in Jupiter diameters)	Time of orbit (days)
Io		$1\frac{3}{4}$
Europa	$4\frac{1}{2}$	$3\frac{1}{2}$
Ganymede		7
Callisto		

INDEX

abrasion   13
Andromeda   62
aquiclude   48
aquifer   48
artesian basin   48
atmosphere   2, 3, 4, 5
attrition   13

basalt   14, 21, 24
Big Bang   46
black hole   37

carbon cycle   3
cepheid variable   62
climate   2
cold front   10
conservative plate margin   22, 24
constructive plate margin   22, 24
continental drift   23, 24, 25, 56
continental shelves   14
Copernicus   43
core   16
coriolis effect   7
cosmology   47
craters   27, 42
crust   16

day   28
deposition   12, 13, 49, 55
destructive plate margin   22, 24
dew   5
discontinuity   19
doldrums   6

Earth   26, 28, 32, 34, 41, 43
earthquakes   16, 17, 19, 24, 50, 58, 59
earth structure   16, 20
ecliptic plane   32
ellipse   32
epicentre   17, 50, 58, 59
Equator   29
erosion   12, 14, 49
evapotranspiration   5

faults   16, 17, 22
fog   5
fold mountains   22, 55, 56
fossils   23
fronts   10, 11
frost   5
fusion   37, 39

galaxy   30, 37, 38, 47
Galileo   45, 63

global airstreams   6, 7
granite   14
gravity   31, 34
groundwater   4

Hertzsprung–Russell diagram   38
high pressure systems   9
horse latitudes   6
hot spots   21
Hubble   47
hydrological cycle   4, 5
hydrosphere   4
hydrolysis   2

ice ages   37, 53
igneous rock   14, 16, 60
Io   42, 63

Jupiter   26, 40, 41, 43, 45, 63

Kepler   53

lava   14, 21, 22
light year   30, 62
low pressure systems   10

magma   14, 15, 21, 22
magnetic banding   24
magnetic fields   17, 19, 24
mantle   16
Mars   26, 33, 40, 41, 45
Mercury   26, 41
metamorphic rock   14, 15, 16, 60
meteor   27, 42, 43, 63
mid-oceanic ridge   22
mist   5
Moon   26, 34, 35, 42, 43, 51

Neptune   26, 41
Newton's Law of Gravitation   34
night   28
nitrogen cycle   3

occluded front   10
oceans   4
ocean ridge   22, 24
ocean trench   22, 24
orbits   27, 34

parallax   62
parsec   62
planets   26, 32, 40, 43

plates   16, 20, 22
plate tectonics   20, 21, 22, 23
Pluto   26, 41
Pole Star   28
precipitation   4, 5
Ptolemy   43
Pythagoras   43

regolith   13
retrograde motion   33, 43
rift valley   16, 21, 22
rock cycle   14

Saturn   26, 32
seasons   28
sedimentary rock   14, 15, 16, 60
sedimentation   13, 22
seismic wave   17, 18, 19, 50, 58, 59
shadow zone   18
soil   13
solar radiation   6
solar system   26, 40
star   27, 30, 37, 39, 40, 43
strata   14
subduction   22
sun   4, 6
sunspot   37, 45
supernova   37, 39
synoptic chart   11
synoptic symbols   9

tectonic cycle   20, 21, 22, 56, 57, 58
terrestrial radiation   6
tides   35
transport   12, 13, 49, 50, 54, 55

Uranus   26, 41

Venus   26, 41, 45
volcano   14, 16, 21
volcanic islands   22
Voyager   26, 42

warm front   10
water cycle   4
weather   2, 6, 8, 11
weather maps   2, 11
weathering   12, 13, 14, 49, 50, 60, 61
Wegener, Alfred   23
white dwarf   39

xenolith   16